Keith Abraham has pinpointed a great need gap in our business world. Our people matter! Passionate people make better performers, which in turn creates a better business and ultimately increases the bottom line — it is that simple!

— **Ed Santamaria, President Rock Tools, Sandvik Mining**

Keith Abraham is the Prince of Passion. I have worked with Keith for over a decade. He has shared his energy, sense of humour and business acumen with hundreds of my team in different countries. The feedback is always exceptional, citing personal insights and providing tools that have led to life-changing transformation. I can attest to this personally.

— **Ian Blair, General Manager,**
Retail Banking, Westpac New Zealand

Keith Abraham is an incredible and credible adviser and presenter. He has a genuine passion for helping people improve themselves professionally and personally. He has ignited a passion in me for 'just getting on with it' and shifting my focus from having a job to having a passion. A great bloke doing amazing things.

— **Jordan Hawke, Executive General Manager,**
Adviser Distribution, Asteron Life

We know if our people are connected to what they are passionate about in their personal life and they have a plan to achieve their personal and professional milestones, then they will be outstanding in their work and for our customers. That is why Keith Abraham's approach to Passion was so right for our people, our customers and our business.

— Lindy MacPherson, General Manager,
Organisational Development & Human Resources, Data#3

Keith Abraham is a unique and passionate guy who has the ability to unleash the potential in any organisation or person. In my experience with global and local companies, we can often spend considerable sums of money to get consultants to find solutions, whereas Keith brings all this thinking and more without the cost, making this book unique and accessible to everybody.

— Chris Beer, President — Asia Pacific, Luxottica

I have often shared a platform with Keith Abraham. He is a big picture thinker, communicates with simplicity and clarity, understands today's technology, and embraces the new technology with his time-tested techniques to engage people. A very passionate man.

— Max Walker AM, keynote conference speaker,
best-selling author, AFL player and Australian test cricketer.

IT STARTS WITH PASSION

BE YOUR
BEST

IT STARTS WITH PASSION

**Do What You Love
and Love What You Do**

KEITH ABRAHAM

WILEY

First published in 2013 by John Wiley & Sons Australia, Ltd
42 McDougall St, Milton Qld 4064

Office also in Melbourne

This edition first published in 2019 by John Wiley & Sons Australia, Ltd

Typeset in 12.5/14.5 pt Arno pro

© Keith Abraham

The moral rights of the author have been asserted

A catalogue record for this
book is available from the
National Library of Australia

Internal images by Brooke and Aimie Dorratt, Dorratt Design

QR codes by Eyeconit Ltd

Printed in U.S.A. by Quad/Graphics.

V224516_022519

Disclaimer
The material in this publication is of the nature of general comment only, and does not
represent professional advice. It is not intended to provide specific guidance for particular
circumstances and it should not be relied on as the basis for any decision to take action
or not take action on any matter which it covers. Readers should obtain professional
advice where appropriate, before making any such decision. To the maximum extent
permitted by law, the author and publisher disclaim all responsibility and liability to any
person, arising directly or indirectly from any person taking or not taking action based
on the information in this publication.

One of the greatest gifts you can give someone is permission and encouragement to dream, to be themselves and ultimately for them to live their passion. To my wife Kristine and daughters, Mazana and Isabella, thank you for this wonderful gift of support and endless belief in my chosen journey. You inspire me to be the best me I can be!

Contents

Preface

**NOTHING GREAT HAPPENS UNTIL SOMEONE
BECOMES PASSIONATE ABOUT SOMETHING!**

This is one of my favourite quotes. Think of anything that has been achieved in the world. It may have stemmed from a need, an injustice, a set of unfair circumstances, an opportunity or an idea whose time had arrived — but a passionate person or a group of passionate people brought it into reality.

If that is my favourite quote, then this is my favourite question: What are you passionate about in your life? What floats your boat? What energises you? What excites you? What gives you your greatest joy? My belief is that life is too short to live without passion, and it is too short to go through the motions or to just exist. Yet how many capable and clever people just exist? They have given up on their dreams, hopes and desires and use the excuse that they have to earn a living, provide for their family and be a responsible adult.

Here's a newsflash: You can do all this *and* live a passionate life. I believe that your responsibility is to be the leading example for everyone who is connected to you. Now, it is not always your fault what happens to you, but it is your choice what you do about it. So what are you passionate about?

This book is about providing a catalyst for those people who are ready to have more, be more and achieve more for themselves, the people who mean the world to them and the community they are a part of. This book has been specifically designed for those who want more out of life, who want to be more in their life and who want to live a more passionate life. They want more than just to exist — they want to live, love what they do and do what they love. So the question is simple — is this you? Are you ready to live a more passionate life?

DO YOU WANT MORE?
MORE THAN TO JUST EXIST, DO YOU WANT TO LOVE WHAT YOU DO AND DO WHAT YOU LOVE?

I have written this book to inspire, instruct, improve and inform you on your journey to discovering what is important to you, what matters to you, what is meaningful to you and what makes a difference to you.

Enjoy the journey.

Keith

About the author

Keith Abraham has become the world's premier thought leader on passionate performance and building passionate based cultures.

Through his work over the past 18 years inspiring people around the world to live more passionately, he has assisted individuals and companies alike to create over 12 million goals.

As best-selling author of three other books and founder of the remarkable global movement the One Goal Global Challenge, he has become a source of inspiration to hundreds of thousands of people through his programs.

As founder of Passionate Performance Inc. he has been dedicated to researching, training and working with people to help them find their passion, harness their passion and turn their passion into personal and professional capital. He has developed a client base of over 265 companies across 20 countries including industry leaders Toyota, Toshiba, Lexus, Westpac, Bupa, NAB and AIA.

Having been presented with the highest honour for professional speaking, the Nevin Award, Keith was also named

'Keynote Speaker of the Year' by the Australian National Speakers Association in 2012.

Keith's life purpose is to leave an everlasting legacy that will make a profound difference to individual lives.

Introduction:
The four parts to creating a passionate life

Most people want certainty in their lives. They like to know where they are going and what is possible for them to achieve. They want to live a life that is meaningful by doing work that matters and by making a difference to the people who count for them.

Meaningful – how to create certainty in your life

Everyone needs to find meaning in what they do and in the role they play in their life, their business, their career and their community. As individuals, we need to understand the connection that comes from the alignment of our purpose, passion and personal goals.

**WHEN THE WHY BECOMES CLEAR
THE HOW BECOMES EASY!**

This one statement encapsulates the premise of the whole book. It is the basis for turning the goal-setting process on its head, leaving the conventional, oh-so-yesterday approach to achieving and finding a bold new way to be more, achieve more and have more of what's important in your life.

In the first part of the book, we discover the power of harnessing the one to three driving emotions each of us has — the power that forms the foundation on which all our successes are built. When people identify the magic of their personal positive driving emotions, the by-product is a laser-like focus and a level of satisfaction that becomes self-perpetuating.

Milestones – how to gain clarity in your life

Dreams and desires are the foundation, but it is the *clarity* that comes from a set of clearly defined milestones that truly transforms intentions into actions. What is measurable becomes attainable. The clarity of a person's milestones allows them to measure their progress and impact.

As will be shown in part II, aligning your emotions, mindset and actions creates an unbreakable personal connection. This connection is created by an easy-to-remember process...

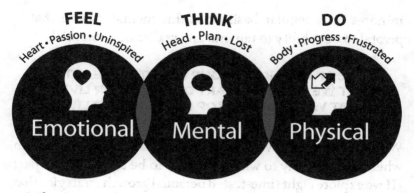

When you start to set goals based on how you want to feel, and establish your key milestones along the way to gaining that feeling, then in taking the physical action your goals become achievable faster through an effortless level of activity.

It is this simple process that turns someone who is uninspired, lost and frustrated into someone who is passionate and making planned progress. As you create certainty you gain clarity. To gain clarity you must have confidence. With confidence comes the ability to let go, certain that your goal will be achieved, which allows you to take the required action.

Mindset – how to enhance confidence in your life

Rarely is it a person's level of ability that stops them from achieving their goals, dreams, desires and ambitions. Most often they are held back by their lack of confidence and belief in what's possible for them, what they're capable of achieving and whether they are worthy of that level of success — this becomes the prison people build for themselves.

On our life's journey each of us needs to become a living example of a person who is certain, has clarity and believes in our ability to achieve our goals, both personally and professionally. And we need to strengthen and reinforce this mindset on a regular basis. It is this mental muscle that is pivotal to our ability to tap into and realise our potential.

ALL OF US KNOW IN OUR HEART OF HEARTS WHAT WE NEED TO START DOING IN OUR LIVES & WHAT WE NEED TO STOP DOING IN OUR LIVES.

We just need to be given the hows to transition ourselves from where we are today to where we want to be tomorrow. In part III we explore eight time-tested personal growth strategies that become a vital catalyst for removing your emotional shackles, mental roadblocks and physical excuses. My goal is to assist you in creating a level of confidence that will allow you to let go of your goal and focus on your intention, relinquishing the worry of whether the goal will come true — and making it happen in your life.

Momentum — how to live consistently in your life

Motivation is *so* '80s. Life is not about how motivated you are; it is about how much *momentum* you have behind you. With momentum you can achieve the unthinkable and the impossible in your life. It is about making the transition from being consistently inconsistent to becoming consistently consistent in your attitude, actions and attributes.

It is about an evolution of self, not a self-imposed short-term revolution. The 'one per cent concept' is about taking small incremental steps that are easy to implement over a period of time. This type of action, taken consistently, will move you closer to your goal and to the type of person you want to become. This improvement concept works, as it minimises the mountain of excuses most people have and diminishes the fear of failure, the fear of success and the fear of change.

Anyone can react and respond; when you are in flow, however, you become the one who is proactive and progressive rather than reactive. You take on the philosophy that *a good plan started today is better than a perfect plan started tomorrow.* As part IV shows, creating real momentum in your life becomes the catalyst that recharges, refocuses and replenishes your soul, spirit and sense of purpose.

MOMENTUM IS NOT ABOUT MAKING MAJOR CHANGES ALL THE TIME; IT IS ABOUT MAKING SMALL INCREMENTAL CHANGES OVER A PERIOD OF TIME.

Taking control

The last thing we need is more information, yet we all need to gain better insights from the information we have. Over the past 27 years I have been a student of passion, high-performance results, the setting of goals and how people go about achieving their goals. During that time I have gained many interesting insights that I'll share with you in this book.

My belief is that before we lead anyone in our business, career, community or family, we need first to lead ourselves. A good friend of mine, Lawrie Montague, once said to me ...

'Either you will set your own goals or you will be part of someone else's goals.'

Discovering our passion, purpose and life plan is one of those great opportunities each of us has to take back control and to focus on the controllables in our life rather than the uncontrollables.

How often do we lose focus, sweat the small stuff and get tied up in issues we won't even remember in a month's time?

If there is one insight I have gained, it is that when we pursue our passion the world has a habit of giving us access to an express lane to our goals. All we need to do is be clear about it and focus on it.

If you knew me personally, you would know that I am practical and a realist, so of course I know you will still experience challenges, roadblocks and circumstances that will slow you down from time to time. That is all part of the journey and the lifelong lessons we need to learn along the way.

I also know that most people want certainty in their life. The only way you gain certainty is to create clarity, because with clarity comes greater confidence in your ability to produce the results you want, and with that confidence comes a level of consistency that leads to certainty. And that is what this book is all about — certainty, clarity, confidence and consistency. If you want to improve, increase or develop any of these four elements, you are reading the right book at the right time of your life.

It Starts with Passion is a book packed with insights, supported by in-depth research, easy-to-understand concepts, visual models that will add to your existing knowledge base, inspirational stories that will engage you, and practical 'how to' ideas you can apply to your own set of circumstances to make real transformational change in your life as you rediscover your dreams, create your goals, explore your life's purpose and pursue your passions.

Part I
Meaningful: creating certainty in your life

CHAPTER 1
Find your way

It is not what or how or when or where that is important. What really matters is WHY you want to do something in your life or seek to achieve a goal. The premise of this book, the foundation for a great life, rests on this quote:

When the why becomes clear the how becomes easy!

When you are clear on *why* you want to do something, you will find *how* to do it or often, in some strange and mysterious way, the how will find you. You will meet a person who knows a person, or you will read an article that gives you an idea about how to achieve your goal.

The challenge is that most of us don't start with the *why*; we start with WHAT we want — and all too often we stop at the what. We don't progress any further or even go after a lot of whats. The challenge is that after some time our soul and spirit require that we pursue what is meaningful and what really matters to us.

**WHY COMES AFTER WHAT.
THE WHAT IS WHAT YOU GO FOR
WHEN YOU ARE DISCOVERING YOUR WAY.**

Think of it like this. When you were a kid leaving school or a young adult at university, everyone would ask you, 'So what type of job do you want? What are you going to do now? What career are you going to pursue?' Later in life, when you are employed or pursuing your own business, people keep on asking you *what* questions: 'What project are you working on now? What is your target for the month? What do you want to achieve this year? What is your career goal?'

Rarely does anyone ask you why. My belief is that the whats that make up our lives result from our search for the why. Our whats are what we do when we are looking for our why. The challenge for most of us is that we stop at *what* because it is easy to measure — we don't have to think about it as long as we do when trying to determine our why. So we get stuck at what, as it is easy to find in status, titles, material gains, financial milestones and comparisons with how well our friends and colleagues are doing. *How* is what we need to do to get to our why.

For each of us, the why represents our reasons, what's important to us, our life's purpose. It's about what matters most to us — our core values that form the fabric of our being. The why, in part, is what we stand for and what we want to be known or famous for as we live a meaningful life.

WHY RELATES TO YOUR PASSION, PURPOSE, REASON, DRIVERS, DESIRE, VISION, BIG PICTURE & INTENTION.

Your why is that one thing that is wanting, and often waiting, to burst out of you. It is the passion that you have put off as everyday life has taken over and consumed you. It is what is in your heart, that voice telling you that this is the right thing to do both for you and for those around you, yet sometimes it is hard to determine as there is no logic to your thinking.

I am not saying you will achieve nothing if you are not clear on your why. You see, when you are focused so much on the *what* you will achieve a great deal, more than most people in your circle of friends, family and colleagues. But after a time you will wonder *why* you are doing it. You will experience a weird sense of unreasonable disenchantment. You know you have achieved and are still achieving, so why are you feeling so disillusioned, disengaged, disappointed or detached? You don't have any right to feel that way! Compared with others you are doing so well, you really don't have any logical reason to feel this way, and yet you do.

WHAT RELATES TO THE SPECIFIC GOAL, THE CLEARLY DEFINED OBJECTIVE, THE DESIRED TARGET & THE ACHIEVABLE MILESTONE.

Once again, deciding on your why is infinitely harder than determining what you want or how or when you are going to achieve it.

HOW RELATES TO MECHANISM METHOD, STRATEGY, TACTICS, PROCESS, MILESTONES, BLUEPRINT OR PLANS.

Why tends to depend on an emotion-based decision that reflects your true self, the essence of you as a person. *What* is logically based and is determined by your thought processes, past experiences and learning from those who have gone before you. *How* is about action, making progress, implementing ideas and being open to attaining rather than just thinking about the goal. *When* is the timeframe within which you desire to achieve the goal. Look at it this way ...

Most people rarely cross the mental and physical divide that exists between *what* their goals are and *why* they really want them. Let's face it, most people don't set goals for the week, month or year, and now we are asking them to determine *why* they exist — their purpose — and the contribution they will make to those close to them, those who know them and those who may never know them but will benefit from their legacy.

WHEN RELATES TO THE TIMEFRAME YOU SET FOR ACHIEVING IT.

It is not that people don't want to discover their why; rather, either they don't allow themselves the time to indulge in what is possible or life becomes too all-consuming to take time out to sit down and think about the big picture. The idea of doing this can be daunting and it is far easier to become busy being busy. And those few who are not sure where to start take the easy road of not doing it at all.

When I interview passionate people for my blog or listen to people from the stage, a common theme permeates their language: 'I always wanted to...I knew I had to try...this one thought dominated my thinking since I was a kid... I dreamt about it all the time. I always knew I would pursue this goal.' Industry leaders, global leaders, great scientists, designers, inventors, innovators, artists, musicians, Nobel or Pulitzer prize-winners, or Olympic gold medallists are all very connected to their why and their reason.

Why is not just confined to individuals. Companies need a big why to engage, enthuse and energise their people and their customers. The companies and entrepreneurs that impress us are those that seem to have a big why, that noble purpose that connects us to their brand or product.

Businesses, like people, sometimes lose their way, though. Their noble purpose — their why — either becomes diluted or is disregarded, or people become disenchanted. At other times people and businesses achieve their why but have not taken the time to refocus on what comes next — what's my why now?

So what is your why? Why were you put on this planet at this time? Why do you want to live a great, meaningful life, a life that is bigger than you, a bigger why than the one you have right now?

CHAPTER 2
Creating real wealth

For most people money is important. It gives them choices, options, and provides them with a certain type of lifestyle. I believe real wealth is a combination of three key components, which I call external wealth, internal wealth and eternal wealth.

External wealth is measured by what you have, whether that be your employment, business title, community status, money in the bank, the type of suburb you live in, what you own, the interests you pursue or even the car you drive.

Most of society measures people using this one criterion; however, such achievement or wealth does not guarantee happiness or overall life success, whatever that may mean for you. In my travels I have met very wealthy people who are surrounded by the trappings of success and appear to the outside world to be high achievers without a worry in the world, yet they are miserable and unfulfilled in their life.

Internal wealth is measured by how much you like yourself. It is about self-love — that ability to like who you are, what you are doing and the difference you make. This type of wealth is not measured by a balance sheet or bank account. It is measured by how you feel, how happy you are, how much love is in your life and how filled with joy you are right now. Perhaps life for you just feels right!

The final component, *eternal wealth*, is measured by what you do for others. It is about the legacy you leave for others to enjoy, the benefits you create for others, the values you pass on to those who know you personally and to those who know you from afar. It is about the gifts you create and leave for others to benefit from both while you are alive and after you have gone. It is not necessarily about creating a foundation or trust, but about creating a legacy that is bigger than you, outside of you and will live on after you.

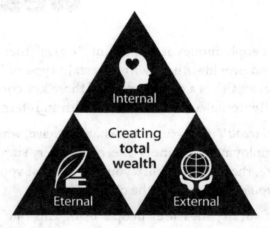

If you want to explore this idea further, ask yourself these questions:

» *External wealth:* What material wealth and success do you want to achieve in your lifetime in order to feel secure, happy and fulfilled?

» *Internal wealth:* What do you need to achieve as a person to feel a greater level of self-love?

» *Eternal wealth:* What legacy do you want to create for others to enjoy and benefit from both while you are here and when you are gone?

CHAPTER 3
Be out of balance to be in flow

So often gurus tell us to find a balance in our life, but what does that really mean? Eight hours' sleep, eight hours' work and eight hours' fun? I'm not sure if balance can be achieved through time allocation; however, it can be achieved by taking small, incremental steps that create a state of mind — a feeling of being in flow.

What do I mean by being *in flow*? It is best explained as the feeling you have when everything is working out for you. Goals are achieved with a greater sense of ease, even a feeling of effortlessness. One opportunity leads to another and that leads to another, which ultimately opens a door for you to attain a goal you had previously had no idea how you could achieve. It is a set of circumstances that manifest themselves in your life, connecting you to the right person and moving you forward and closer to your next milestone.

It does not mean you have no challenges, but you seem to be able to take them in your stride. You are calmer, more composed and find simple solutions that are easy to implement and resolve the issues.

Often what happens is that in hindsight you see or find the reason for the challenge being given to you in the first place. Being in flow means being on purpose, pursuing the goals that are right for you, living the life you have predetermined, and believing you deserve those results.

The opposite to being in flow is being *stuck*.

Have you ever felt stuck in life? Nothing seems to be working for you and every corner you turn reveals another roadblock. Challenges mount up, one after another, and you feel like the whole world has conspired to make your life a living hell. That is what being totally stuck means.

A stuck state does not happen overnight; it creeps up on you over time through the actions you take or fail to take, choices that do not support your being the best you that you can be, achieving more, doing more and gaining better results.

Looking at the figure below, to be in flow you need the scale to be tipped towards the right-hand end.

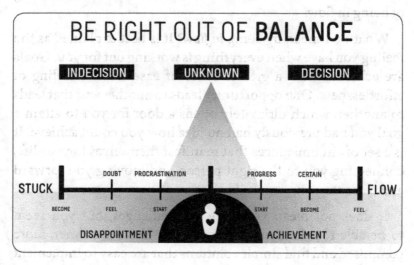

Let's look at why you get stuck and what you can do to get back into flow. You become stuck when you stop making decisions, when you become indecisive, when procrastination creeps in. Procrastination is the greatest contributor to being stuck, because procrastination is the greatest robber of self-esteem and self-confidence.

What you need when making a decision is self-confidence in the choice you make. The problem normally begins when you put off the little things, then bigger decisions, until finally you avoid making any decision for fear of being wrong or facing scrutiny or criticism for the choices you make.

PROCRASTINATION IS THE GREATEST ROBBER OF SELF-ESTEEM & SELF-CONFIDENCE.

Doubt is a by-product of procrastination and a catalyst for undermining self-confidence. When you suffer doubt you feel unsure and start to second guess, and you become reluctant to step out of your comfort zone. A pit opens up that leads you to think the worst, see the worst and believe the worst is going to happen. What you focus on, you create and manifest in your life, so is it any wonder that you feel and experience the challenges you do?

Let's talk about doubt for a moment. How do you act and feel when you are consumed by doubt?

Take a moment and think about how you act and feel when you are doubtful. Now do any of those feelings empower you? Do any of those feelings propel you closer to your goals and dreams? Do they bring out the best in you?

You have a choice on how you feel. Your state of mind, and how you want to feel, is controllable by you. In fact, it is one of the few things in this world over which you have total control, if you choose to. So how do you take back control and get into flow?

You need to make some decisions. Life is about making decisions. All through this book I will ask you to make decisions. Now understand this: every decision you have ever made was right — for that time and that place with the knowledge you had at the time, it was right.

TAKE BACK CONTROL & GET INTO FLOW.

Two minutes later, two hours later, two weeks later, two months later or two years later, it might not have been the right decision. However, we don't live in the future. We plan for the future but we don't live there.

Make a decision, and if it is not the right one then make another. Get into the habit of making decisions if you want to make progress. As you can see on the scale on page 12, it is about making progress, because that is what leads each of us to certainty.

It is not about being perfect; it is about making progress. Too often people wait until everything is perfect before they start; this is just another form of procrastination. If you want to beat procrastination, stop thinking about finishing the task or reaching the goal, just focus on taking action that gets you started. A great friend of mine, Malcolm McLeod, says...

'A good plan started today, is better than a perfect plan started tomorrow. Your goal is to get it going, then you can get it right!'

If procrastination eats away at your self-confidence, progress is the greatest enhancer of self-esteem and self-confidence. From action and confidence comes a greater sense of certainty. I don't know about you, but I like certainty in my life. It's about knowing where you want to go and knowing how to get there. How do you act and feel when you have certainty in your life?

What is true for you? Take a moment to think about how you act and feel when you are certain.

Wouldn't you like to have those feelings more often and more consistently? These are feelings that put you into flow and keep you there, and they all come from taking action, taking little steps that edge you closer to your goal, your desired state of mind and the life you want to lead. I am not saying your life is going to be perfect, but you will like it more and you will like who you are!

HOW OFTEN ARE YOU CONSISTENTLY INCONSISTENT?

CHAPTER 4

The 6 emotions of achievement

I have been fortunate to have spent much time over the years talking to thousands of people about their passions, purposes and plans. For me it is always interesting to see where people are on their journey towards their goals. I have identified six different mindsets that people fit into when it comes to setting and achieving goals. I have seen first-hand their mindset around how they feel about achievement, the characteristics they display when they are achieving, and the mental lassoes they entwine themselves in as they achieve their goals or don't. Let me share with you some of these insights to help you determine your own position at this moment in your life.

We have all experienced these six emotions in some form or another as we have moved through life. Achievement is a double-edged sword: it can inspire us to go to the next level or it can cut the ground from under us as we reflect on what we could have done or could have been.

There are five mental lassoes that limit us as we seek to achieve our goals and dreams, and there is one mindset around achievement that I call *the certain* that we all need to work towards to live a passionate, productive and positive life.

The certain

The opposite of certainty is doubt. Doubting yourself, your abilities and your sense of worthiness is the first stage in a downward spiral towards feeling disappointment and despair.

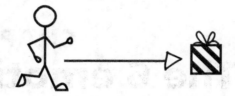

All of us want more certainty in our lives. Certainty is the sense of knowing that this goal will be reached, that this action will lead me one step closer to a meaningful milestone in my life. With certainty comes greater confidence, and with confidence comes a belief that things will work out for the better. You know in your heart that you are in flow and that flow is taking you ever closer to your desired goal.

When you are certain, you know what you want to achieve and have a plan with clearly defined steps to take. You are under no illusions: you know it will take energy, effort and enthusiasm to achieve the goals. You also understand that there will be challenges, that there will be roadblocks along the way and you will need to take some unplanned but necessary detours, but you are certain that these goals will be achieved.

People who are certain can be recognised by their high degree of clarity, confidence and control, which generates momentum as they pursue their goals. This momentum seems to propel them even faster and more effortlessly towards their objectives; things just go right for them. Some may call it luck, some divine intervention; for others it can be best summed up in the unattributed quote, 'The whole world steps aside for the person who knows where they are going.'

So do you have certainty in your life when it comes to your direction, relationships, career, business results and finances? Are you living each day with certainty? Becoming certain is the goal for all of us to work towards. If you don't feel certain about your future, then let's discover where you feel you are situated *now* and in the next chapter I will suggest a way in which you can move forward as you pursue your passion, purpose and plans.

The lost

Have you ever felt lost? As though you were moving but not making any progress? Perhaps your life seems to be passing you by. You are travelling through life but you don't seem to be arriving at any particular destination. Your direction is dictated by life, circumstances and other people, rather than being created and then pursued by you.

How do you tell if someone is lost? I ask people, 'What do you want to achieve?' The response is often 'I don't know.'

'What do you think you're achieving at the moment?'

'I don't know.'

'Tell me what you have achieved in the past.'

'I don't know.'

If you don't know where you have come from or what you have achieved in the past, you don't know where you are in your life at the moment and you don't know where you are going next — that is a good definition of lost!

Feeling lost in your life is a draining emotion. The more lost you feel, the more lost you become, and the more you will doubt what is possible. Most of these people don't know what they want to do or have never taken the time to think through what they really want to achieve. They have become busy being busy; rather than taking control of where they are going, they have allowed life to consume them.

Because doubt has gained a firm foothold on the mental muscle to dream of what is possible, these people never stop to think about what could be achieved and who they could become, so they live with doubt daily. These people are recognised either by their low level of self-confidence or by their excessive overconfidence (even when they know everything is *not* okay).

They are often defeated before they actually start, and just as they begin to think about what they could achieve, their subconscious kicks in to remind them of their past failures and how comfortable it is to put up with mediocrity. Because mediocrity produces less disappointment, less to worry about and less expectation of you by those around you.

Do you feel lost?

The frustrated

Ever been frustrated with yourself? You know you are capable of achieving more but for some reason you just don't feel like you are moving in the right direction. You don't feel like you are making any progress. I believe frustration is the opposite of progress. I know for myself I experience the greatest levels of frustration when I feel I am not making progress even though I am taking action. This comes from the fact that you know what you don't want but don't know what you do want. Can you relate to this?

The conversation I have with some people goes something like this:

'What do you want to achieve?'

'I don't know, but I know that it's not this! It's not this job I'm doing or the relationship I'm in or these financial circumstances I have.'

My response is simple: 'Okay, what do you want then?'

'I don't know!'

You can feel the frustration in their voice and the anxiety in their whole being. If I was to dish out some tough love, it would be to say, 'If *you* don't know what you want, then you deserve what you've got.'

The truth, however, is that these people are suffering from living in the past while being consumed with their present circumstances, and rather than thinking about what they are capable of achieving they are focusing on what is *not* right or *not* working for them. For these people, a mind shift is required before a physical result can be obtained. They need to understand that their past does not determine their future. They need to break the mental cycle of believing they can only achieve what they did in the past by beginning to dream again. You see, it is hard to live in your past when you are focused on the future.

Do you feel frustrated?

The confused

Have you ever known what you wanted but had no idea how to achieve it, or been unsure where to start or what the right steps to take were? If you feel like that now, you are probably experiencing some confusion.

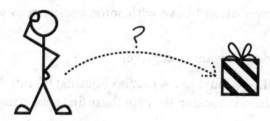

People who feel confused know the goal they want to achieve. Defining the steps, strategies and solutions they need to implement to achieve their goal is the challenge. It is not what to achieve, but *how* to achieve it that is causing them confusion. These people have a desire and a dream but sometimes lack the knowledge of how to turn their dream into reality. While it is not as bad as feeling frustrated, confusion can be very restrictive, because when you don't know what to do, you tend to do nothing. The challenge is that these people are looking for the *right* way, rather than *a* way. Perfectionism creeps in and rather than making progress towards their most important goals, they wait for everything to be perfect before they start.

If you are confused, your goal is not to try to get the plan right — your goal is to *get the plan started*. Then you can get it right. Taking action is the solution. Now is the time for progress, not perfection, because if you wait for perfection, you will never get started. Creating momentum in your life could be as simple as just taking a single step or action, making that first move. If you are focused on taking the first step, life has a habit of showing you the next step to take, and the next and the next. Create momentum towards a goal you desire and the plan will unfold around you.

Do you feel confused?

The unclear

Ever had too many choices? With so many opportunities to pursue were you unclear which was the right one to take? If you are experiencing that situation in your life right now, you are most likely feeling unclear. You are trying to determine which is the right choice for you right now.

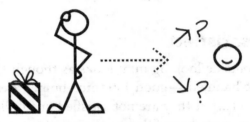

A typical admission by someone who is unclear about the right goal they should pursue in their life, career or business goes something like this: 'I have this opportunity to pursue this role in this organisation, or I could go back to school to gain a degree in this discipline, or the company I am working for now has a new role working overseas in this country. I am unclear which one I should go for.'

So how do you think most people respond?

When there are too many opportunities most people choose to wait, rather than to start. Remember how Edison described genius as '1 per cent inspiration and *99 per cent perspiration*'. You will be inspired as you take action, gain momentum and make progress.

Most people ponder, pontificate and procrastinate as they weigh up the pros and cons in search of a solution. They start to second guess their gut instinct and get stuck in a paradox of perfection paralysis — waiting for all the planets to align in their life before they take their next action or pursue their next goal.

It is not that these people have not succeeded in the past. They have often achieved great results. It is just that they are daunted by the question 'What should I do next?' My belief is simple: no opportunity is right or wrong, but some have a greater degree of right than others. So rather than picking the 'right' one, you just need to pick one and make it right for you. Remember, it is only an opportunity if you take advantage of it.

The unsatisfied

From the outside looking in, it looks as though these people have got it handled — good job, nice home, great holidays, high achiever... but they are not satisfied or fulfilled. There is a void that has not been filled by their past achievements and regardless of what goals they set and achieve they do not hit the mark. The common solution for these folks is to set bigger goals, work harder, strive more and be better. They tend to focus on the next what. But after a while it just doesn't cut it anymore and the feeling of being unsatisfied takes root in their mind, body and spirit.

These people usually find it difficult to discuss their feelings or current mindset because most other people don't get that this person could have anything to be concerned about, and it is sometimes easier to keep up the charade than to address the internal circumstances and lose their credibility.

The challenge for these individuals is to find their true purpose, to discover their real goals, and to pursue a life that is bigger than them, that is outside of them and that will live on beyond them. In other words, it is achieving goals that gives them a sense that they are not just accumulating money, material possessions or meaningless titles.

This is a hard merry-go-round to get off, as you don't want to give up the success you have! It is a matter of identifying what is important to you now. What does meaningful work look like to you? What passions do you want to pursue still? People love what they do but they are not *in* love with what they do. It is not a matter of quitting, selling up and having a sea change; it is just about falling back in love with your life, with who you are, what you do now and what you want to do next.

Which mindset do you most identify with?

Each of us has experienced all six of these emotional mindsets at some stage during our working and home lives. You may be experiencing one emotional mindset in your work life at the moment while experiencing another in your home life. This is where doubt starts to creep into your perspective. For any change to occur the first step is to identify where you are right now. Then you can apply one of the six transition solutions that will move you forward towards certainty and beyond, which is what we will discuss in the next chapter. Read on!

CHAPTER 5

The 6 ways to create certainty in your life

Now you know where you are emotionally when it comes to achievement in your life, let's discuss the solutions that can move you from here to where you need to be to create a greater degree of certainty in your life. Even if you are 'certain' now, I want to share with you one strategy that will move you closer to your goals in less time.

The certain

It's great that you are certain about what you want and how you are going to achieve it. The key for you now is to remain focused on your goals so that those goals are realised in the shortest time and with the least effort.

The easiest step in the goal-setting process is deciding on the goal; the hardest thing is to remain focused on it. There are so many distractions in the digitally connected, 24/7 world in which we work, live and play. Here are three actions you can take to remain focused on what matters to you:

1. Develop a mindset that means you always focus on the things that count.

2. Ask yourself the question 'What's important now?'

3. Write down your goals on a card or create a list of your goals on all your digital devices, then read those goals every day to keep them in the front of your mind.

I recently listened to a speaker colleague of mine, Nic Stewart, sharing an experience he'd had in Los Angeles during a dinner with Sir Richard Branson. When Nic had an opportunity to ask him a question about goal setting and how often he read his goals, Sir Richard said he believed millionaires read their goals 1 to 17 times a day and billionaires read their goals 19 to 29 times a day. For himself, Sir Richard reads his goals on average 21 times each day.

I know from the feedback we receive from people who have attended our Passionate People Program that if people read their goals once a week they achieve four to six goals out of ten in the course of the year, but if they read them each day they achieve seven to nine goals out of ten during the course of the year. I also took this away from this story: reading my goals so often stops me thinking about all the reasons I cannot achieve them.

As a side note, Sir Richard then showed the small group of people dining with him his goal journal in which he had listed 645 goals. I believe Sir Richard Branson is a living example of someone who has created, and lives with, certainty.

The lost

The solution is simple: make a decision, then make another one. Start to take small steps, make small improvements, then decide to be better and take greater action.

Why don't people make decisions?

Fear!

Here are the three great fears that stop people from making decisions, along with some of the most common rationales behind why people give way to these fears:

» *Fear of failure.* What if I make a decision and it does not work out for me? What if I get labelled by people? What if people make fun of me? What if I'm wrong?

» *Fear of success.* What if making the right decision means people have a higher expectation of me from now on? What if I can't live up to that success in the future? What if I was just lucky the first time?

» *Fear of change.* If I make that decision, what would I have to change to be able to make it work for me? What if doing things differently from now on was uncomfortable and inconvenient?

What is holding you back from tapping into your potential and realising your possibilities? What is one decision you need to make today that will move you from lost to certain?

The frustrated

If you are frustrated, your solution is to decide what you don't want. Sometimes it is easier to decide what you don't want first. So write down everything you don't want in your life — all the things that do not serve you well, that annoy or frustrate you, everything that needs to change. Once you have done that, define what the opposite of each item is for you. If you don't like the role you have at work, identify what you don't like about it. It may be working with numbers, when you really want to work on creative concepts or design. If you have a business that requires that you deal directly with lots of people, and you don't actually like working with people, then maybe you should consider an internet-based business that involves much less face time. If you don't like managing a big team of people, maybe you should be outsourcing your needs or hiring a manager so you can focus on the work you love to do.

I have consulted to many businesses where we have given the business owner or CEO permission to go off and do the work that matters and is important to them, only to see their business flourish while they too are happier, which may help explain why it grows and prospers!

What do you need to let go of or reverse in your life? What do you not want and what is the opposite of that for you? Knowing there is an alternative gives you hope for the future.

The confused

Confusion exists when you don't know how to get from point A to point B. You know what you want but you are unsure of how to achieve it. The solution for you is to design a plan with a coach or mentor or someone you trust.

Collaborate with someone else as you work out what you need to do to achieve your goal. They will be able to ask some of those tougher, more clarifying questions:

- » Why do you want to achieve that goal?
- » What do you think the first step is?
- » Have you thought about this approach?
- » What roadblocks are stopping you at the moment?
- » If you took this action, what do you think the consequences would be for you?
- » Who else do you need to gain assistance from to achieve your goals?

—A.S.K.—
ASK; SEEK; KNOW. ASK QUESTIONS, SEEK A RESPONSE, KNOW HOW TO APPLY THE INFORMATION.

Many more questions could be asked — that is the power of having someone else work with you. They will look at your situation with fresh eyes and from a different perspective.

You know the answers, but you need someone to ask you the right questions to create greater clarity for you, and with clarity comes certainty.

Who do you know that you could work with to assist you in creating your plan to reach your goals?

The unclear

Recognising that you have so many opportunities, the key is not picking the right one but connecting with your heart. The solution, if you are unclear, is to follow your heart. Forget about what you think is the 'right' goal; focus on the goal that is screaming out at you to pursue it. When you follow your heart, success, money, love and joy will follow you. Take the money out of the equation. What does your heart tell you to do or to pursue?

Do you understand, they can never pay you enough money to do the stuff you hate to do? The money is great but you are still miserable. Someone once said (and it has always stuck with me): 'What causes an ulcer is not what you have eaten, but what's eating you!'

How do you follow your heart? First write down all the opportunities you currently have. Ask yourself, if each opportunity involved making the same amount of money, which one would give you the greatest joy? Which one would you love to do most? Rank them from the greatest joy to the least joy. Then stop and meditate on the list by being still and listening to your intuition. Finally, note down the opportunity you connect with the most.

We all make mistakes but for me, rather than focusing on what could have been or should have been, I ask myself what I learned from it and what I would do differently next time. I also carry one thought in my mind when I reflect: everything is perfect! Even if it was not the perfect outcome, what could I learn that will better equip me for the future? When I look at it that way, everything *is* perfect!

The unsatisfied

You have achieved so much, but at this point you are thinking to yourself, What else do I need to do to feel fulfilled in my life? What is my next challenge? You may find that what you have been doing doesn't engage you as it once did. You may find the challenge has gone out of your personal or professional life and feel like you have been cruising of late.

You need to find a better reason why — a goal that is bigger than you, that is outside of you and that will live on after you. And you need to create a *manifesto*. A manifesto is a public declaration of what you intend to do, a document that identifies your vision for your life, that defines what is important to you, what matters to you and how you are to make a difference.

Austin Kleon includes a great manifesto in his book *Steal Like an Artist:*

> **Draw the art you want to see, start the business you want to run, play the music you want to hear, write the books you want to read, build the products you want to use — do the work you want to see done.**

My life's work manifesto is to ...

» do work that matters and makes a difference

» write, create and speak about how people can be better, do better and have better results for themselves and their family

» have meaningful conversations with people about what is important to them

» show anyone who is interested how to discover their passion, pursue their passion and live with passion.

What is your manifesto? If doing what you are doing is not floating your boat or motivating you or energising you to become a better you, then you need a bigger reason why!

CHAPTER 6

How people lose their passion

An age-old question asks, are leaders born or made? I think they are made through a set of circumstances and situations that flicks a switch and brings out the best in them. So does the same apply to passion?

I don't believe so. I believe we are all born passionate and at some stage during our life either we fuel the fire or we let it die down to nothing. I look at my two daughters and see the passion in their eyes for the things they love to do. I see adults who after so many years reconnect with their passion and get a second lease on life with energy to burn regardless of their age.

So how do people lose their passion? My take on this is that our lives are divided into four areas ...

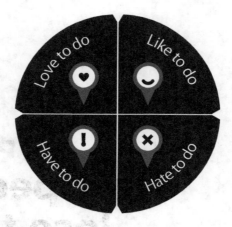

There are things in our life that we *love to do* — the things that give us the greatest joy, that we are passionate about, that energise us, that recharge our batteries. Then there are things that we *like to do*. These things give us pleasure, but we are not as passionate about them as we are about the things we love to do.

There are also things in our life that we *have to do* to reach a goal or achieve an outcome. They don't give us much joy or energy, but we know that it is all part of the process and the price we need to pay to get things done.

Finally, there are things in life that we *hate to do*. If we had a choice we would avoid doing them; we might delegate or even outsource these tasks. One way or another they have to be done, but they are a pain and a drain on us.

Now I am not saying you should stop doing all the things that you have to or hate to do, but I do know that when people lose their energy or passion it is because they have nothing in the first two categories of this model, 'love to do' and 'like to do'. The simple act of completing tasks in these two areas gives us the ability and energy to tackle the uncomfortable and the inconvenient; it recharges our batteries, restores our spirit and passion for life so we can push through and do those things that don't give us joy.

You know when people are flat and unenthused and have lost their zest for life. My prescription is simple: what do you love to do?

WHATEVER IT IS FOR YOU, GO & DO IT!

Most of the time the reason people are not pursuing their passion is because of the story they have sold themselves. They come up with excuses, like 'I don't have time'. Get this: you will never have time! It is not about having time, it is about making it a priority, it is about making a deliberate choice. You will never get back the time you spend on doing the things you love to do; however, you will get back the energy, the love and the joy so you can do more with the time you have.

My belief is that we all have a battery that sits inside us and if we don't recharge it from time to time, it will go flat. This could manifest itself in your becoming sick or just tired and drained.

WHAT IS IT THAT YOU LOVE TO DO? PURSUE THAT! DO THAT! THEN LOVE WILL FOLLOW YOU! JOY WILL FOLLOW YOU.

CHAPTER 7
Reconnecting with your passion

What are you passionate about? This is my favourite question, as I have found it's a great way to start a meaningful conversation with people. I hope you understand the principle of doing activities and tasks that you love as a way to recharge your batteries and rekindle your spirits. If you still don't know what you are passionate about, that's okay. Some people have suppressed their passion for so long it's hard to define what it is anymore.

It's all okay! The answer is always in the questions we ask ourselves. In my Passionate People Program, which is a day workshop we conduct all around the globe, I have the workshop participants answer a series of questions that clarify their passion or purpose and what they have to do to make it a reality in their life. (You can go online at www.passionatepeople. com and download these questions and do the exercise for yourself.)

1. *What are you passionate about in your life? What do you love to do?*

This is not about writing down just one passion; list at least three to five passions. When I ask this question, many people list their family as their passion, and so do I. I am passionate about my wife and daughters. My second love is the work I do. I am really passionate about working with people to discover and pursue their passion and live a passionate life. My third love is photography and my fourth is travel. Now what I really love is when I can combine all four loves.

2. *If the money was handled in your life, what would you love to do with your time, energy and skills?*

   Not how would you spend the money, but what you would do with your time. Some people would do what they have always done — same job, same role, same routines. That's okay. There are no rights or wrongs in this activity.

   What this question does is give you the opportunity to dream of how you would choose to spend your time, what type of meaningful work you would do, and the difference you would make to those people who mean the world to you and those people you may not even have met yet.

3. *What do you need to change in your life in order to achieve all that you are capable of achieving?*

   After almost two decades as a professional speaker the one thing I have learned is that the audience always knows the answer. I just need to ask the right questions and create the right environment for them to discover the answer for themselves. So I believe you know in your heart of hearts what you need to change. Identify the three things in your life that are holding you back.

4. *What do you need to focus on in your life right now to make you happy, satisfied and passionate?*

As I have already suggested, it is what we focus on that counts. What is it that you need to focus on right now? Maybe it is getting to base camp in your life, such as getting healthy, finding your mojo again, repairing a broken relationship or just creating the space to do what is important.

5. *What advice would a 95-year-old give to you?*

   Imagine you are 95 years old and have lived a great life, and someone your age now, just like you, turns up at your door. They seek your advice on how to be a better person, a better professional, a better leader, and how to have a better life. What advice would you, the wise 95-year-old, give to the person you are today about what is important and what is not so important, what matters and what doesn't, what counts and what doesn't count? What advice would the older, wiser you have for the person you are today?

6. *What do you believe is the noble purpose in your life?*

   These are not your everyday, run-of-the-mill questions. They have been designed to make you think. Henry Ford once said: 'Thinking is the hardest work there is, which is probably the reason why so few engage in it!'

   Robert Byrne gave us these words...

'The purpose of life is a life of purpose.'

What is your purpose? What do you want to be famous or known for? I am not talking about being famous like a movie star, but famous in the hearts and minds of the people in your life who matter. Your answers to the following questions will form the basis for your purpose now.

- » What matters to you in your life?

- » What is important to you in your life?

- » What do you want your life to stand for?

- » What type of work would give you the greatest meaning?

- » What do you want to do that would make a difference?

It's all about making you think, stretching your mind so you can have a more meaningful conversation with yourself and those people who mean the world to you. To follow your heart you first need to know what is in your heart. These questions will lead you to find out what is in your heart.

TO FOLLOW YOUR HEART YOUR FIRST NEED TO KNOW WHAT IS INSIDE YOUR HEART.

CHAPTER 8
What's the big picture for you?

Have you ever had the opportunity to visit Disneyland? The last time I went I purchased a book called *WALT ... The story of Walt Disney*. The seed for Disneyland was planted when Walt would take his daughters, Sharon and Diane, to an amusement park or to Santa Monica Pier on the weekend.

Disappointed with the dirtiness of their facilities and how they were operated, he thought there must be a better way for families to connect and have fun together. It was this idea that inspired him to dream a dream that has made 630 million people happier, including a number of us reading this book.

For Walt Disney that initial seed soon bore fruit. In 1953 he purchased 160 acres of orange groves and walnut trees south of Los Angeles. Walt drew up his plans and costed out his dream and then went about securing the funding to turn his dream into a reality. In 1953, $17 000 000 was a lot of money, and do you know what? It still is today! So Walt, in his best suit, his grand plans under his arm, a clear vision in his head and passion in his heart, approached the first bank.

Now I'm not sure just how the conversation went, but you could imagine that after he had made his pitch with enthusiasm, the exchange was most likely something like, 'So what you want to do, Mr Disney, is to bulldoze the income-producing orange and almond trees on your 160 acres an hour and a half outside LA and build an amusement park that you hope people will come to?'

'Yes!'

'You are crazy! No!!!'

The second bank said no, the third said no, and the fourth ... bank after bank said no. In fact, 462 banks and financiers turned him down. The 463rd, however, said, 'Yes! We are just as crazy as you!'

Construction started and Disneyland was built within 12 months. On 18 July 1955 Disneyland opened for the first time. At 43 degrees it was one of the hottest days on record — so hot the bitumen laid the day before melted! They expected 6000 people to come and 28000 people turned up. The following day they expected 25000 visitors and 50000 people turned up. In the first year their expectation was for a million guests to pass through the turnstiles, and a million came in the first 90 days. With this success old Walt thought, 'I could be onto something!'

From landlocked Anaheim, California, Walt and his brother Roy decided to spread their wings and purchase over 30000 acres in Orlando, Florida, making the acquisition under a number of different company names so the land prices did not escalate. The dream was to start building the next Disneyland. Unfortunately Walt passed away on 15 December 1966, but the show must go on!

On the opening day of Walt Disney World, 1 October 1971, Roy was asked to walk the media through before the guests were allowed in. It was during this walk that a journalist made the comment, 'Isn't it a shame Walt never got to see this park open?' Roy stopped in his tracks, looked the man in the eye and said, 'The reason why you and I see it today is because he saw it first!'

He saw it first! Before we can ever achieve anything in the real world, you and I first need to have a vision in our hearts and minds. Most people's definition of a long-term goal is Friday! What is your big picture for your life?

YOU & I NEED TO HAVE A VISION IN OUR HEARTS & MINDS FIRST, BEFORE WE WILL EVER ACHIEVE ANYTHING IN THE REAL WORLD.

CHAPTER 9
Creating your life to-do list

The best activity I can give you is to write down 100 goals you want to achieve in your lifetime. People often call this a 'bucket list'. When a doctor gives you six months to live and you decide to write down all the things you want to do before you kick the bucket — that's your bucket list! One of the best ways to discover what is important and meaningful in your life is to complete the '100 Goal Challenge'.

For me it started when I was 23 years old. At school I was academically challenged, not a high achiever at all, and at 15 I dropped out. I didn't know what I wanted to do with my life so I took the first job I could get. I began as a labourer and got a job working for Klaus, a 6 foot 4 inch German bricklayer. Klaus was a record-holding brickie who could lay bricks faster than I could get them to him. After six weeks I thought to myself, 'I have to be smarter than this job. I can't do this for the next 40 years,' so I took the easy option and went back to school.

School didn't get any easier for me. I just got worse at it until one day my mum said I was wasting my time at school and suggested I get a job. Mum asked me what I wanted to do and my response was, 'I don't know!' Mum was solution oriented, but aren't most mums? She had a lot of push in the local council — she was the tea lady. She got me my first real job working in local government with Albert Shire Council in the Water Supply and Sewerage Department, the bowels of the organisation! I was well motivated to get out of Water Supply and Sewerage, and I worked my way up to the Health Department and the prestigious position of Noxious Weed Inspector. After six years in that role my boss came to me one day and asked if I'd like to go on a week-long leadership training program called RYLA — Rotary Youth Leadership Award. Now you have to understand that I was unmotivated, lazy and bored. Then he said the magic words: 'You get a week off work with full pay,' and I thought to myself that maybe I was leader material after all. Maybe I was a leader and didn't know it! This leadership program was the catalyst I needed, and it turned out to be a defining moment in my life.

It was a great week filled with inspiration, information and insights. On the last day the program leaders asked us to find a shady tree and take the time to write down 100 goals we wanted to achieve in our lifetime. We were given 90 minutes for this activity and as I sat there thinking about everything I could do in my life — my dreams, my goals, my desires and my passions — I was able to list just six lifetime goals. Reflecting on this I thought my life was going to be either short or very boring! The seventh goal I wrote down was to finish the list and get to 100. It took me six weeks to complete the challenge, but over the past 27 years I have completed it five times. If you'd like to check out my current list, just visit www.passionatepeople.com.

There are still some goals from my first list that I have not yet completed, but lots of others that I thought would never be possible for me to achieve in a lifetime were realised within six months of writing them down. People ask me why 100 goals. Because anyone can write down 10 or 20 things they want to do in their lifetime. To list 100 you have to think, you have to dig deep to bring to the surface all those things you have pushed to one side. This is the task I set business leaders who have lost their passion and energy, their mojo, because it ignites the spark of *what could be* and *what if* in your mind.

Are you up for the 100 Goal Challenge? To get you started I would like you to think about the seven areas, noted below, that make up the dreaming process and to ask yourself the seven questions that follow. Now find yourself a quiet place with a journal or use your smartphone or the tablet app that can be downloaded from www.passionatepeople.com. All you need to do is to list some of your dreams.

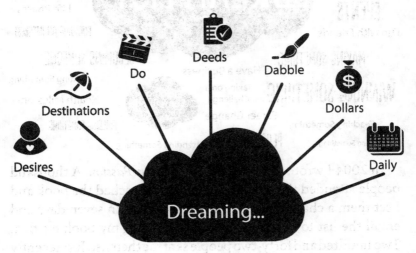

Here are the questions you need to ask yourself:

> » What do I *desire* to achieve?
> » What *destinations* do I want to visit in my travels?
> » What type of person *do* I want to become?
> » What *deeds* would I like to do for others?

» What hobbies have I *dabbled* in that give me great enjoyment?

» What are my *dollar* goals and financial position, and what money milestones do I want to achieve?

» What do I want to do *daily* with my time?

Think about all the things you could do ...

In 2004 I wrote a book titled *Living Your Passion*. A thousand people attended the conference where I launched the book and I set them a challenge: write down 100 goals in seven days and email the list to me, and I would send them my book for free. Two hundred and forty-two people sent me their list. Just recently I was in Perth, Western Australia, to deliver a presentation. At the end a man approach me and identified himself as Murray, one of the 242 people who had sent their list to me back in 2004.

Murray told me he had achieved most of his goals, but the four he shared with me were that he had started his own optometry business, learned to play the trumpet, joined a band and travelled to France to find the grave of his great-great-uncle's father, who lost his life in the First World War. Murray played the Last Post over his forebear's grave and had just got back from Gallipoli, where he attended the Anzac Day dawn service.

Dreams do come true, but you need to write them down. I was so blown away by all the things Murray had achieved that I asked my office to contact the other 241 people from 2004, attaching their original list of dreams. What happened next was truly amazing. We started receiving emails from people with comments such as ...

'I had forgotten all about this list, but I have achieved 50 of the 100 I wrote down.'

'Thank you so much for this — I had forgotten all about it! Can I submit a new one for the next 5 years? Some things on my list make me laugh now. I have achieved over half of what is on there, probably more like 60–70%, which is pretty amazing since I had completely forgotten about it! Most importantly I live by my personal goals these days almost 100% ... I am so thankful you have sent this back to me!'

'Great to hear from you and see your blog each week. I am doing well at work and I am working on those 100 goals I want to achieve. I have bought and set up the Harley Davidson motorbike for touring, started to teach myself Asian cooking and built a woodworking shed. It's a work in constant progress and coming along well. I've bought a digital camera and am using it as well. We bought a home on 1/2 an acre and fully renovated it in 2009.'

'I am slowly working at this and it surprises me that until you made contact I hadn't looked at the list for some time, but have achieved some goals. Hope all is well, Keith, and live life with passion.'

'Since the challenge was issued to write down a list of 100 goals, it is quite satisfying to see how many have been attained. I have bolded those 25 attained and underlined are the two that are no longer goals. One that I attained last week was to ski in the NZ Ski Masters at Coronet Peak in

Queenstown, where I raced the Downhill. I surpassed all my expectations by winning it. At speeds over 100 km an hour, a huge adrenaline buzz. Thank you for issuing the challenge. Writing these goals down has had a great subliminal effect.'

You need to have dreams! So take up the challenge and set yourself 100 goals you want to achieve in your lifetime.

CHAPTER 10

Lifetime dream examples

In the previous chapter I mentioned that 242 people sent to me their lists of 100 goals. For a long time I just kept them in an electronic file on my computer. After a presentation people would often tell me they were able to write down 20 or 30 or 40 goals, but they struggled to get to 100. So I thought I would create a document that could act as a catalyst for people seeking to complete the 100 Goal Challenge.

I wrote an e-book with 400 examples of goals that you can review, use as thought provokers or copy in eight key areas. The e-book is called *Discover Your Passion* and you can download it from www.passionatepeople.com.

Here are 200 examples you can look at right now to assist you as you create your own Lifetime Dream List and take the 100 Goal Challenge:

FAMILY

1. Surprise my partner with a weekend away.
2. Have family and friends over for a dinner party monthly.

3. Travel every year to visit family members overseas.

4. Call family and friends on their birthdays.

5. Take children on an annual family holiday.

6. Organise my school reunion.

7. Each year complete a personal development program with my children.

8. Shout Mum and Dad a trip around the world.

9. Trace my family tree.

10. Frame the family pictures I adore.

11. Reconnect with my brother and sister.

12. Record my children laughing and having fun.

13. Take pictures and video of my family.

14. Organise a weekend away with a group of family and friends.

15. Take my partner on a date weekly.

16. Teach my children to cook.

17. Teach our grandchildren about our family history and traditions.

18. Write a book about my life for family.

19. Take my family to where I grew up.

20. Organise a reunion of all my old friends.

21. Reconnect with some of my distant friends.

22. Travel around Australia for two months as a family adventure.

23. Take every opportunity to build my children's self-confidence.

24. Pay for my children's education at a great school.

25. Take my family overseas on a 12-month exchange program.

TRAVEL AND ADVENTURE

1. Visit 100 countries in the world.

2. Live for three months in a winery in Italy.

3. Run the New York Marathon.

4. Learn to tango.

5. Learn to surf in Hawaii.

6. Attend a Burning Man festival.

7. Go to the winter and summer Olympics.

8. Go on safari in Africa.

9. Go to Antarctica.

10. Go trekking in Nepal.

11. Travel through Vietnam by bike.

12. See a Broadway show in New York.

13. Visit the Taj Mahal.

14. Visit the top five art galleries in the world.

15. Buy a motorbike and ride around Australia.

16. Sail around the Greek Islands.

17. Snorkel on the Great Barrier Reef.

18. Visit Easter Island.

19. Trek to Machu Picchu.

20. Go to La Tomatina tomato fight festival.

21. Whitewater raft through the Grand Canyon.

22. Go on a western cattle muster.

23. Have dinner at the top of the Eiffel Tower.

24. Watch a sumo wrestling match in Tokyo.

25. Run with the bulls in Spain ... with someone slower than me!

COMMUNITY

1. Donate money to an orphanage.

2. Volunteer in the children's ward of a hospital.

3. Volunteer to help feed the homeless.

4. Sponsor a family living in a developing country.

5. Volunteer overseas using my talents and skills.

6. Give regularly to a charity I am passionate about.

7. Clean out old and unused things and give to the needy.

8. Develop a community retreat for people to visit and recharge their batteries.

9. Set up my own charitable foundation.

10. Volunteer with an existing foundation to help injured wildlife.

11. Make someone smile each day.

12. Go on a fun run to raise money for a worthwhile cause.

13. Sponsor a World Vision child.

14. Create a businesswomen's networking group.

15. Counsel young men on becoming a father and all it entails.

16. Read to the elderly in nursing homes.

17. Create an annual event that raises awareness of a needy

cause in my community.

18. Get involved in a disadvantaged youth development.

19. Register as a bone marrow and organ donor.

20. Teach others to build wealth.

21. Join a local group involved in environmental issues and assist them in planting trees.

22. Sponsor a sporting team for local kids.

23. Donate money to a local cause anonymously.

24. Write a book about life skills, have it printed and give it away to different groups.

25. Organise a Christmas street party to get to know all the neighbours.

LIFESTYLE

1. Challenge my comfort zone by getting involved in some new activities.

2. Create a space in my home or garden to be creative.

3. Spend some time in my hammock reading and relaxing each week.

4. Schedule time to paint.

5. Buy a holiday house to escape the city.

6. Plant and maintain a garden.

7. Design, plan and build the home of my dreams.

8. Buy myself fresh flowers once a week.

9. Keep a journal of five things that make me happy each day.

10. Do activities that make me laugh out aloud each day.

11. Treat myself to a manicure or pedicure once a month.

12. Schedule 'me' time every day.

13. Own a weekend café.

14. Learn to play a musical instrument.

15. Cook or bake a different dish once a month.

16. Build a piece of wooden furniture for my home.

17. Write a children's book.

18. Design a piece of jewellery and have it made.

19. Publish a book.

20. Design and build a cubby house.

21. Meditate for 20 minutes each day.

22. Walk along the beach or through bushland.

23. Find and pursue a new hobby.

24. Go on a two- or three-day retreat once a year to refocus on my life work.

25. Take time out to do the one thing I love to do each week.

PERSONAL GROWTH

1. Create a positive legacy for others to benefit from.

2. Become a better time and priority manager.

3. Learn to speak another language fluently.

4. Do my master's degree.

5. Learn to sing and play a musical instrument.

6. Participate in an acting course.

7. Learn self-discipline through meditation.

8. Improve my vocabulary, spelling and grammar.

9. Find a mentor to ensure I achieve all my goals.

10. Interact with people who support my vision.

11. Learn to cook.

12. Study the creative arts.

13. Participate in a photography course.

14. Attend a wine appreciation course.

15. Learn reiki and involve myself in yoga.

16. Complete a weekend course that involves my passion.

17. Research nutrition to better look after myself.

18. Attend a personal growth seminar once every quarter.

19. Discover the job that I'm best suited to.

20. Schedule time to myself to reflect on achievements.

21. Settle any past disputes or conflict with people.

22. Every six months spend two days by myself reflecting on the past and planning out my goals for the next six months.

23. Study, work and live overseas for 12 months.

24. Write a book that enhances the self-confidence of children.

25. Create a personal development program and deliver it to key people.

BUSINESS AND CAREER

1. Use my current business skills to help others.

2. Make a firm career decision and pursue it.

3. Help clients make goals and realise them.

4. Get involved in learning opportunities that work offers.

5. Build a great network of contacts in and outside my industry.

6. Write a manifesto for my business venture.

7. Acquire board positions in organisations that interest me.

8. Become the managing director of a company.

9. Be headhunted for a job.

10. Coordinate and implement a marketing plan of my own design for a business.

11. Cut down on my hours at work: achieve a better work–life balance.

12. Get my small business venture off the ground.

13. Be well regarded and respected in my chosen industry.

14. Earn at least $200 000 per annum.

15. Become a manager within the next 6 to 12 months.

16. Develop a realistic business plan, implement the plan and follow it through.

17. Turn my hobby into a profession that generates a profit.

18. Release a best-selling music album.

19. Find a job that will help me reach my full potential.

20. Grow my business to be number one in my market.

21. Design programs of development for potential leaders.

22. Assist 10 people to become successful in their career.

23. Own a multinational company.

24. Facilitate an innovation conference to change the shape of my industry.

25. Start a part-time online business that generates a full-time income.

FINANCIAL

1. Make a profit on the stock market.
2. Pay off my credit card debts.
3. Own my own investment property.
4. Help my kids get started with a house deposit.
5. Pay off all outstanding debts.
6. Get my superannuation strategy working better for me.
7. Save 10 per cent of my income for future investments.
8. Learn more about how to reduce my mortgage.
9. Buy 10 investment properties in the next 10 years.
10. Invest in an overseas holiday villa.
11. Create a personal budget.
12. Be financially secure in my retirement.
13. Pay off my mortgage.
14. See a financial planner to organise a financial plan.
15. Become financially independent in the next 10 years.
16. Buy a house within two years.
17. Have a million dollars in the bank.
18. Be able to afford to travel the world whenever I want to.
19. Save for quality items, not quantity items.
20. Learn about the workings of my personal finances.
21. Learn basic accounting skills to run a small business.
22. Create or invent a product that generates a passive income.

23. Build my dream home.

24. Teach my children how to save, invest and create wealth for themselves.

25. Read one investment or wealth-creation book every year.

HEALTH AND FITNESS

1. Become 100 per cent healthy, fit and energised.

2. Reach my ideal weight and stay there.

3. Ensure I have regular health checks.

4. Do yoga every week.

5. Walk for 30–60 minutes each day.

6. Learn to rollerblade.

7. Limit my intake of unhealthy foods.

8. Participate in a team triathlon.

9. Swim on average three times a week.

10. Run a full marathon.

11. Join a group of people who are interested in the same types of exercise.

12. Eat more raw fruit and veggies and more fish.

13. Get a personal trainer.

14. Join a slow food group.

15. Give up smoking.

16. Research the best type of fitness for me.

17. Educate myself in nutrition.

18. Do the stretching exercises my chiropractor and physiotherapist recommend.

19. Build my upper body strength.

20. Go on a 10-kilometre fun run.

21. Learn how to cook healthy, tasty meals for my family.

22. Have my body checked out for any early signs of cancer.

23. Look into alternative medicine as part of my health routine.

24. Pick one fitness routine and work on it for a month.

25. Live to be a happy, healthy 100-year-old.

Now create your own list of the 100 Lifetime Goals you want to achieve!

Part II
Milestones: creating clarity in your life

CHAPTER 11
S.M.A.R.T. goals don't work!

They work for companies but not for people, because we are emotional creatures. That's why I think S.M.A.R.T. (Specific, Measurable, Attainable, Realistic, Timeframe) goals are dead. The idea is so 1980s! It's time for a new way to set goals for the different times we live in, and for the different ways we can all achieve what is important to us.

The reason I believe the S.M.A.R.T. idea is past its use-by date is that you and I experience a vast range of feelings and emotions. There are over 130 different emotions we can all experience.

After 25 years of working with people and their goals, I believe the missing piece of the puzzle is the emotional connection, the true goal alignment that comes when you know how you want to *feel*, you *think* about what you want to achieve and then you *do* what's necessary to make it come true.

Why would logical, intelligent people set a goal that is important to them, that will bring them a better result, only to procrastinate over taking the action, and have to negotiate with themselves each step of the way?

Traditionally people approach goals like this: they set the goal, take action to achieve the goal, achieve a result, then experience a feeling — joy, success, satisfaction or accomplishment. It looks like this:

1. *Goal:* I want to lose 10 kilos.

2. *Action:* I exercise more, eat less, take vitamin supplements and limit alcohol consumption over the next two months.

3. *Result:* I do this for long enough and consistently enough to lose the 10 kilos.

4. *Feeling:* I feel more energised, have more confidence and experience a sense of success.

Now this is logical. However, a logical connection does not compel us to take action. It validates the action, but it doesn't motivate us. The challenge is that because we don't achieve immediate success or we make only limited progress, we begin to question the benefit of making the effort. Our subconscious plants seeds of doubt because our focus is on losing 10 kilos, not the feeling we can experience moment by moment, day by day. We fall into the trap of focusing on the goal or outcome, rather than the activity that carries us towards the goal.

So why don't we invert this model and start with how we want to feel? Each of us is driven at any one time by one to three emotions.

Let's start with how you want to *feel*, whether that is across your lifetime, this year, this week or just today. Then let's determine what *action* you have to take today to achieve that feeling. From there you gain a *result* that leads, step by step, towards the achievement of your overall *goal*.

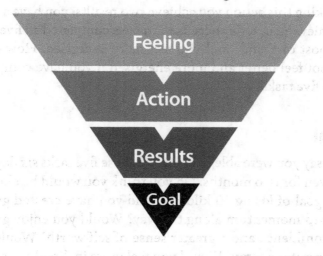

Feeling

Let's look at it in real-life terms. Let's say you want to feel energised. It is important to you to feel you have the vitality to achieve all the things that are important to you and still have energy to burn. You have determined that being energised is one of your driving emotions. Later I will show you how to determine your top three driving emotions — it is such a simple yet profound process.

Action

You decide that to feel energised today you need to drink two litres of water, exercise for an hour, meditate for 15 minutes, eat the healthiest food option for you (whether that is a protein breakfast, three serves of vegetables, or fruit and nuts for snacks during the day), and achieve three personal or career objectives each day.

Results

By taking this action you achieve two results: you have a sense of achievement today because you have completed all five tasks (or most of them); and you feel more energised. How could you not feel better and more energised if you have completed these five tasks?

Goal

Let's say you were able to complete these five tasks six days out of seven for two months. Do you think you would be closer to your goal of losing 10 kilos? Would you have created greater forward momentum along the way? Would you enjoy greater self-confidence and a greater sense of self-worth? Would you have greater energy? Would you feel more inclined to keep up this ritual because you are making progress towards your goal?

The real value is that you have stopped focusing on what you are not achieving, letting go of the pressure that an unfulfilled goal can create in your mind, and started to focus on what you can do today. We all feel better when we feel like we are making progress!

Think progress, not perfection.

IT IS NOT ABOUT BEING PERFECT, IT IS ABOUT MAKING PROGRESS.

CHAPTER 12
Driving emotions

As I mentioned in the previous chapter, we all experience many different emotions. We feel hurt, we feel love, we feel joy, we feel sadness. Depending on what research you read, these could number up to 135 or 177, with eight so-called core emotions. So for this purpose we are simply going to say there are many to choose from. Some people feel a hundred of them in a week; others no more than 10 in a lifetime.

Most of the time, however, you and I will experience up to three driving emotions that sit high above all the other emotions. Our emotional hierarchy looks like this ...

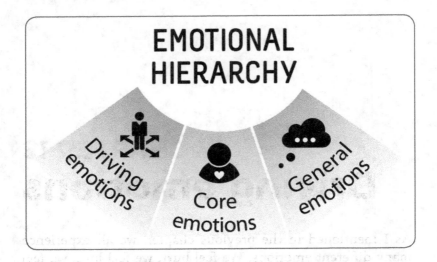

Your driving emotions

These three driving emotions animate us, motivate us and connect us to our goal by propelling us towards the results we want and desire. Whether it is acceptance or love or acknowledgement, these are the emotions we crave, sometimes to our own detriment. Whatever driving emotion propels you to be the best you that you can be, you need to combine it with high self-confidence, self-worth and self-belief. Over the next couple of chapters I will show you a simple way to determine what is truly important for you to feel, have and do.

Your core emotions

These are the emotions that you experience day by day and week by week. They define your natural persona, whether that is happy, organised, caring, conscious or focused. Sometimes they are positive and uplifting for your spirit and soul; at other times they are the emotions that undo you, the negative emotions that bring out the worst in you. You know when it is happening. You may be under pressure, unsure, tired or committed to something you don't believe in. Unfortunately it is hard to stop these emotions from coming to the surface.

Your general emotions

These are all the rest of the hundred-plus emotions you may experience. Maybe you experience some of them only once, and maybe you never want to repeat the experience! They can be positive or negative, and some of these emotions may be 'out of character' for you.

In his book *The 7 Habits of Highly Effective People*, the late Dr Stephen Covey developed the metaphor that we all have an emotional bank account with everyone we have a relationship with, an account based on trust rather than money. When we keep promises and commitments to them we make a deposit in their emotional bank account that builds trust, rapport and credibility. When we make a promise or commitment that we fail to keep, we make a withdrawal from their emotional bank account. The same is true of us as individuals: when we achieve a goal (which is a commitment to ourselves in the truest sense), we make a deposit in our personal emotional bank account, as it strengthens our driving emotions and gives us a feeling that is a reward in itself.

The goal itself is not the only reward you can experience; neither is the feeling you have when you reach those milestones along the way. It is okay to reward yourself for achievement and effort. So often people set a goal, work their brains out to achieve the goal but then don't celebrate. They just get back in the saddle and do it all over again, setting another goal, working their brains out to achieve it...you get the picture. The by-product of this is that sooner or later your subconscious asks itself, 'Why am I doing this?'

That's when you lose the motivation and drive you once had. You wonder why you are no longer energised by life or the task at hand. What is the opposite of this? You achieved something great three years ago and you are still celebrating, living off past glory. Yesterday's hero! Time to get off it and get on with it!

So take the time to celebrate, but don't stay celebrating that achievement forever. What is an appropriate reward? It might be taking time out to do something you love to do, one of your passions. It could be a celebratory dinner. It could be taking time to reflect on what you have achieved and what you have learned along the way. It could be sharing your success with people who matter to you, or it could even be a physical reward or specific predetermined prize or gift.

I often use this quote...

People respond best to reward and recognition. Rewards along the way will bring out the best in you. More importantly, they will do so in a more consistent, sustainable and conscious way.

CHAPTER 13
Feel – Think – Do ... true goal alignment

The power of an emotional connection is amplified when you combine it with a mental connection and then with a physical connection. When true goal alignment is formed you no longer simply set goals; you create goals that are true to you, connected to you and aligned to you. The challenge for some people is that they know what they want but not why they want it, or they know what but they don't know how to achieve it, or they know what and how without understanding why.

In reality, the *what* is what we go for when we are discovering our *why*, and unfortunately most people get stuck at the what. Think about those questions people asked you at school: *What* are you going to do when you leave school? Think about at your work: What is your target for this month? We are all so focused on what that we never explore the why, and yet the why is where the reason, the emotion, the purpose and passion live. It is the source of our energy, our desire, our drive and our determination.

Achieving goals is more than just taking action. First you need a plan of action; otherwise it is like driving somewhere without knowing your final destination or the milestones along the way. Then, as we learned in an earlier chapter, having a plan and taking action without knowing how you want to feel is like driving the car without a destination in mind and not knowing why you are on the road in the first place.

Feel — Think — Do. The power of this trilogy is unique, yet very few people are aware of it or consciously use it, even though some people use it naturally in an unconscious way. As you read through these next few pages you will learn how to apply it in your daily life.

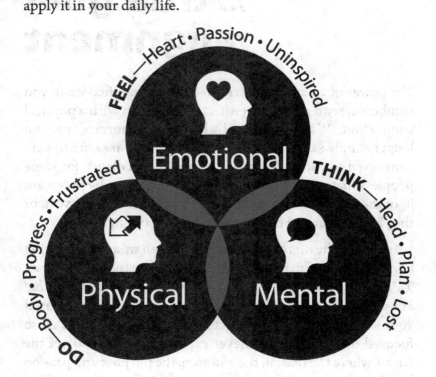

This is why it is critical to create *true goal alignment*. How do you want to *feel* when you achieve this goal? What do you *think*

you need to achieve to reach this goal, and what action do you need to *do* now to make this goal come true?

Feel — Think — Do. Each of us will be stronger in one of these areas. You may be so emotionally connected to your goal that it fills your body with raw energy and enthusiasm. Or you may be a great planner and think a lot about how to achieve your goal. Then again, you may be the sort of person who makes it happen — you just get out there and do it.

However, it is when we combine all three of these elements that we gain the greatest traction. By bringing together our emotional, mental and physical attributes we compound our ability to achieve better results using a whole body approach. We have this super-computer sitting on top of our shoulders so why do we use only part of it to achieve all we are capable of, all that is possible, all that we are worthy of becoming?

Emotional connection

This is where your passion comes from — your emotional connection. It is your reason why. It is about determining how you want to feel, understanding what your heart is telling you. This is about listening to your heart, not just your head all the time. If you don't have an emotional connection with your goal you will feel uninspired, unmotivated and underwhelmed in your life.

If you are emotionally overstimulated, however, you can experience a lack of focus. You may know people who are so excited about their goal and yet they rarely take action towards achieving it! Most likely they are easily distracted by the urgent, rather than the vital, and they become freshly excited about a new goal without even starting to realise the first goal. The Next Shiny Object easily distracts them. They become bored quickly and often suffer from *start/stop syndrome,* starting a task then stopping for no apparent reason.

Mental connection

This is where your plan comes from. The mental connection is the ability to logically and methodically plan the attainment of your goal. In your mind you know what you need to achieve. Your head tells you to do A followed by B and going on to C. You start to map out what action steps you need to take in order for this goal to be reached.

Without a mental connection with your goal you will feel lost, as though you are travelling without a map to guide you or set you in the right direction.

If you are mentally overstimulated, however, you may overplan and overprepare, always looking for the perfect set of circumstances to present themselves before you get started. I call this the *as soon as syndrome*: as soon as I get this new job I'm going to start my saving plan. As soon as the new year comes around I'm going to start the new health and fitness plan I have all mapped out. You may suffer from procrastination — you could even be described as all talk and no action.

Physical connection

This is where progress comes from. The physical connection is about making it happen. It is about taking action, the physical activity you do today to make this goal come true for you. When you don't have a physical connection with your goal you will feel frustrated because you will not be taking action. For you it is all about action and making physical progress, regardless of why you are doing it or whether you have a plan.

If you are physically overstimulated you can be busy being busy all the time. You can get so engrossed in doing the low-value tasks in your home and work life that you cannot see the big picture. You also get stuck in the *work hard, get ahead* syndrome, which means you lure yourself into a false sense of security, thinking everything will work out as long as you work hard.

The magic of goal setting comes into play when you bring all three connections together in your quest to achieve the goals that are most important to you. Here is the formula in summary:

Step 1. *Feel* — Determine how you want to feel this year.

Step 2. *Think* — Design the goal you need to achieve to reach your desired feeling, as determined above.

Step 3. *Do* — Decide what you need to do today, this week and this month to achieve your goal. Think about all the specific action steps you can take that will move you closer to your desired feeling and the goal that will give you that feeling.

Quick *Feel — Think — Do* self-assessment

This exercise will give you a quick understanding of the area in which you are strongest in order to determine the areas you need to strengthen as you create a true personal connection and use the power of true goal alignment. When you are focused on ...

Feel: the goal comes from your heart — it just feels like the right thing to do.

Think: the goal comes from your head — the plans you create.

Do: the goal comes from your body — the action you take.

So are you more emotionally, mentally or physically connected to your goals? Pick which one of the three areas that you think best describes you when it comes to setting and achieving your goals. There are no right or wrong answers, and no one area is 'better' than the others. Tally up your scores in each of the three columns. To harness the power of goal connection we need the power of all three elements working with us and for us.

Feel		Think		Do	
____	Inspired	____	Idealist	____	Initiator
____	Spontaneous	____	Scheduled	____	Self-reliant
____	Talkative	____	Thinker	____	Tenacious
____	Animated	____	Analytical	____	Adaptive
____	Passionate	____	Planned	____	Productive
Total ____		Total ____		Total ____	

Now transfer each column's total score to the pie graph below.

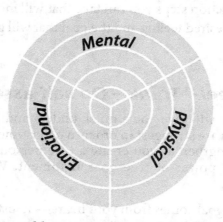

The following table is a simple snapshot of how you may act and react depending on which of the three areas you tend to be stronger in or more focused on in your life.

For example, if you are more emotionally connected to your goals, your greatest asset is the passion you have to pursue them. Your challenge may be that you can become easily distracted. The solution for achieving your goals is for you to maintain a focus on what really counts. Your friends may describe you as excited or excitable. The best strategy for you to move forward is to create a plan to encourage you to make regular progress. Most likely your driving emotions are that you want to feel inspired, energised and passionate.

	Emotional	Mental	Physical
Your asset	Passion	Plans	Progress
Your challenge	Easily distracted	Over-thinking it	Busy being busy
You need to	Maintain focus	Take action	Create strategy
Best described as	Always excited	Always planning	Always busy
To move forward	Plan and progress	Passion and progress	Plan
How you want to feel	Inspired Energised Passionate	Organised Decisive Planned	Proactive Tenacious Focused

When you are strong and consistent in all three areas, you will *attract, adapt* and *achieve* your goals so much more easily.

CHAPTER 14
Putting the Feel – Think – Do process to work

I would like to share with you some examples of the *Feel — Think — Do* process at work and provide some soft-copy and hard-copy downloadable resources for you to use to plan out your key goals using this process.

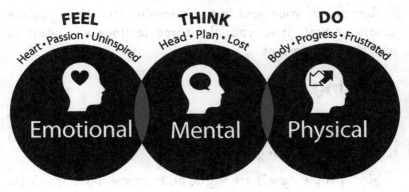

Feeling

The first principle is before you establish what you want to achieve, you need to decide how you want to feel. In the next chapter I will share with you a simple process for determining your three driving emotions. Combining all three driving emotions into one goal creates an even greater connection to your goal.

So how do you want to feel?

Remember, your goal is to determine the three positive emotions that drive you, the three feelings you want to experience every day.

Thinking

Now you need to use your mental muscle to determine the best goal to achieve in order to give you that feeling. The goal needs to be specific and tangible.

Most people's goals are vague and not specific enough for our built-in navigator to set course for this destination. Here are some of the fuzzy goals I see people write down:

'I want to make more money this year than I did last year.'

'I want to be paid a bonus this year by my company.'

'I want to find a new job.'

'I want to complete my course.'

'I want to lose some weight.'

'I want to get fit again.'

VAGUE GOALS EQUALS VAGUE RESULTS.

So they are clearly defined, build your specific goals around some of the following elements:

» *size* (e.g. big, small, height, length, weight)

» *quantity* (e.g. number, weight, money amount)

» *quality* (e.g. attitude, characteristics, knowledge, skills)

» *seen* (e.g. visited, colour, shape, image)

» *position* (e.g. role, title, location, authority)

» *object* (e.g. owned, purchased, obtained, achieved).

Now create a new, comprehensive, in-depth, clearly defined, specific goal statement starting with 'I have', 'I will' or 'I am'.

WITHOUT A SPECIFIC GOAL YOU WILL STRIVE BUT NEVER ARRIVE & SEEK BUT NEVER OBTAIN.

Doing

Everyone has good intentions. It is never about intention but about implementation. It is about taking action, those small incremental steps over a period of time that move you closer to your goal. Most people never take the time to plan out the action steps. What may seem like a mammoth task ahead of them puts people off even starting.

Action fits into two categories — doing a little often, or doing a lot all at once. As you plan out your action steps think about the actions you can take today, those you can take this week, what action needs to be taken this month and even the steps that need to be taken within the next 90 days.

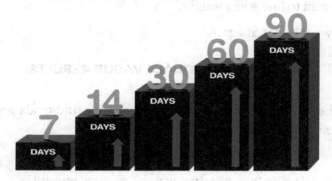

Activity cures inactivity. Take the first step. Pick five actions that will each take you only five to ten minutes to complete. Now it's about creating momentum.

This may not make sense mathematically, but from a psychological point of view the day you take the first step is the day the goal is 50 per cent completed. There may be 100 actions you need to take; however, by the simple act of starting you have created forward momentum and once you have started you are more inclined to take the next step. Starting is always the hardest part!

Here is an example to show how it works:

Feel ... abundant, relaxed, successful

Think ... Pay off my credit card debt of $5000.

Do ...

> *Today* — Make my own lunch. Remove my credit card from my wallet.

> *This week* — Create a personal budget that includes a $200 a week saving plan. Eat takeout only once this week.

This month — Put off non-essential purchases for the month (for example, clothes, big nights out). Make a double payment of the due amount required on my credit card. Visit my tax adviser to make sure I am claiming all the right deductions. Finish reading the book that outlines the 10 ways to reduce personal debt for some additional ideas on saving money.

Let's look at a health and fitness goal.

Feel ... energised and healthy

Think ... Aim to weigh 75 kilograms and become fit enough to jog 10 kilometres non-stop.

Do ...

Today — Walk for four minutes and jog for a minute, and repeat this for one hour. Eat protein-rich food and drink two litres of water. Limit myself to one coffee. Select the healthiest and freshest option for a meal.

This week — Complete the hour-long walk–jog routine for five of the seven days. Eat healthy for six of the seven days (on the seventh I can eat my favourite food as a treat). Weigh myself (my aim is to lose one kilo). Meet with my personal trainer to discuss what other type of daily fat-burning exercises I can do. Check out some health menu options for evening meals. Eat five servings of fish this week.

This month — Aim to jog for 2.5 minutes and walk for 2.5 minutes for an hour five days a week. Lose three kilos for the month. Watch three different YouTube videos about nutrition and weight loss. Find a training partner to jog with three times a week. Investigate running in the local 10-kilometre fun run.

It's as simple as that. You will notice that each action is specific. To assist you further on your journey I have created a number of tools and resources. The first is a worksheet to help you plan out your goals using the *Feel — Think — Do* approach: just visit www.passionatepeople.com or scan the QR code at the end of this chapter to download the worksheet.

Meaningful ... **creating certainty**

Your key goals for this year

Feel ... *how do you want to feel this year?*

Goal #1

Goal #2

Think ... *what goal do you think you need to achieve this year to gain that feeling?*

Goal #1

Goal #2

Do ... *what do you need to do each day and week to achieve that goal and feeling?*

Goal #1

Goal #2

keithabraham.com

"I am my message. It is not what I say, it is what I do."—Mahatma Gandhi

Second, you can download a PDF of this card. This is a handy tool to help you reflect and focus yourself on the things that count when it comes to your key goals. Visit www.passionatepeople.com or scan the QR code at the end of this chapter to download a PDF of the planning card.

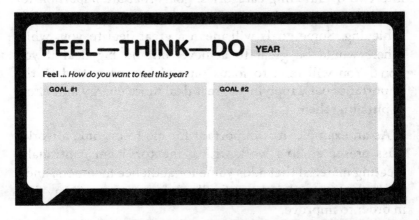

The third item is a smartphone app for your iPhone, BlackBerry or android phone, which you can also find at www.passionatepeople.com or by scanning the QR code at the end of this chapter. The app has been designed so you can use the *Feel — Think — Do* process to plan out your key goals right in the palm of your hand. You will be able to conduct all the key processes presented in this book on your smartphone.

I am often asked if I use this process for all my goals. No, just for the ones that are important to me. You see, your goals will fall into two overarching categories: goals that are *important* for you to achieve, and goals that you are merely *interested* in achieving. Some goals will mean a great deal to you, while others would be great to achieve, but no big deal if you don't. You will tend to focus on and be committed to the important goals, applying a great deal more energy and effort to pursuing them.

As an example, it is important for me to become a world-class presenter, so I work with a mentor, I am continually creating material that adds value for audience members, and I study the best and seek out feedback from experts in my field in order to improve.

On the other hand, one of my lifetime goals is to achieve a hole-in-one at golf. I am interested in this goal. I play, on average, only once every couple of months, but every time I stand on a par 3 hole I think to myself, 'Today could be the day.'

You need to pursue a combination of goals that are important to you and goals you are simply interested in achieving.

CHAPTER 15
Determining your driving emotions

Now that you understand the *Feel — Think — Do* process and the value of goal alignment you are ready to determine your driving emotions — how you want to feel and what that feeling means to you. Take a moment to review the life to-do list that I asked you to create from chapter 9. Now look at each dream or goal you listed and ask yourself this one question: *How will I feel when I achieve this goal?*

Use this emotion cloud as a guide.

Revisit 25 or 50 of your lifetime dreams and see what three emotions keep coming up time and time again. After reviewing a few of your dreams you will notice a trend.

When you feel you have the three positive driving emotions that you most connect with and relate to, and that just feel right to you, then move on to part two of this exercise, which is to determine what each driving emotion means to you.

It's not about finding the right definition out of a dictionary; it's about creating your own definition that suits you, that means something to you. Your definition could be a few words, a number of sentences or a list of bullet points. There is no right or wrong answer; however, the more detail you can put around your driving emotions the more connected you will become to it.

For example, these are my three driving emotions and what they mean to me:

» **Energised**. I have energy to burn every day. I have an endless supply of energy for my family, my clients, my audiences and my friends. I am upbeat, positive and seek out ways to move forward. I take everything in my stride. Everything I do is effortless. I have great energy to overcome challenges, roadblocks and issues as they arise. And my energy is infectious: it engages, inspires and recharges people I come in contact with. My energy is sustainable and self-perpetuating.

» **Impactful**. I am 100 per cent certain of the work I need to be doing in my life. I am a living example of a purposeful and positive person pursuing my passions. I understand my gifts and talents and use them in a meaningful and impactful way. People recognise our excellence and appreciate what we are providing. We assist people to have more meaningful conversations with the people who mean the world to them.

» **Successful**. I know I am making a positive difference in my family life and my work life. I am doing work that matters and makes a difference, and that is important to me. I am creating a positive, passionate legacy for others to enjoy and benefit from when I am gone. I am recognised as a leading expert in my field, a world-class presenter and facilitator capable of moving people to be more and have more in their lives. I take the complex and make it simple and take the simple and make it personally compelling.

The great benefit of setting goals based on emotional drivers first is that it opens you to the potential of so many other opportunities to experience that emotion in your life, because form follows emotion.

You are most likely aware of the axiom *Form follows function*. Hartmut Esslinger, founder of FROG Design, who was contracted by Apple in 1982 to work on the design of the Macintosh Computer, coined the revealing phrase 'Form follows emotion'. By becoming emotionally connected to your goal you help to manifest it. Like begets like, and the happier you are the happier you will become.

FORM FOLLOWS EMOTION.

All goals that are important to you will have an emotional connection. If the goal is important to you yet its achievement has eluded you, then you need to create an emotional, mental and physical connection to it — a connection that has a clear personal *why*, a defined personal *what* it is you're actually trying to achieve and a personal plan for *how* you are going to make it a reality. Let's now explore how you apply this concept to long-term planning.

CHAPTER 16
Mapping out the milestones

There is a difference between milestones and goals. Goals are the destinations we work towards and milestones are the points along the way we use to measure our progress on the journey towards our destinations. We need always to keep in perspective that it is not just about the destination but about the journey. It is not about perfection but about the progress we make, and it is not the results but the actions we take that are often the real gift of setting and achieving goals.

Imagine you are driving to a town you have never been to on a road you have never travelled before. It always seems longer the first time you go there, and it always seems shorter on the return trip. People can tell you how far it is in miles or kilometres or even in hours, but somehow you need those mileage markers or milestones along the way to measure your progress.

When it comes to defining long-term goals, companies and individuals are different. Over the past 10 years I have worked with Toyota and had the opportunity to travel to Japan and meet with senior company executives. It was at one of these informal meetings on a floating junk on Tokyo Harbour that I asked, 'How far in advance do Toyota plan to produce a car for the mass market?' I knew that Japanese companies are famous for having 100-year visions, but the response still amazed me:

'We have working models for cars that we will launch in five years' time, clay models used in wind tunnels for cars in seven years' time and a research facility at Mt Fuji with 2000 researchers working on modes of transport for 40 years from now.'

Just imagine you are a 50-year-old researcher and are working on a project you may not see realised in your lifetime! Now I am not saying you need a 40-year plan, but you do need a plan.

People have differing timeline perspectives when it comes to thinking about their goals. For some people it is easy to think of long-term goals; others find it difficult to think beyond the week ahead. There are people who find it very easy to plan, prepare and produce in the short term; others find it difficult to get down to the detail of what needs to be done today to produce a long-term result in the future. The challenge for all of us is to think about our goals in three timeframes — long-term, medium-term and short-term ...

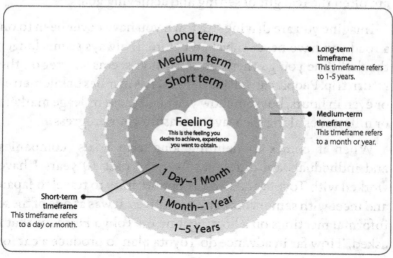

» **Short-term goals**. These goals can be completed in one day or one month, require few steps to achieve and can be reached through short, concentrated effort.

» **Medium-term goals**. These can have a timeline of one month to one year; they often involve a number of tasks, objectives and milestones along the way.

» **Long-term goals**. This is where you start to create your long-term vision. These goals have a timeline of anywhere from one year to five years. Long-term goals need to be broken down into short- and medium-term goals.

The best way to describe these three types of goals is to give you some examples by following one goal through the three phases. So, once again starting with how you want to feel first...

FINANCIAL EXAMPLE

FEEL ... freedom (that comes from being debt free), relaxed, successful.

Long-term goal (5 years): Pay off my mortgage ($150 000 owing to the bank).

Medium-term goal (1 year): Restructure our personal budget to make double loan repayments for the next 12 months.

Short-term goals (90 days): Review with my partner where we spend our money. Look at ways to save money on our bigger expenses — phone, power and personal items. Plan out any major purchases and family holidays for the year ahead. Set my personal career goals so I qualify for my sales bonus at the end of the year. Talk to our friends John and Mary, who have just paid off their home, to find out how they did it quicker than the loan term. Double check with our bank to make sure there are no penalties for paying out the loan and find out if there is a better interest rate for our home loan to save on interest.

CAREER EXAMPLE

FEEL ... accomplished, proud, contented.

Long-term goal (3 years): Become National Director of the Sales and Marketing division.

Medium-term goals (18 months): Complete the MBA from Bond University I started two years ago. Produce consistent above-target results in my current role. Exceed my end-of-year sales target by 10 per cent.

Short-term goals (6 months): Find a business mentor outside my current organisation. Network within my organisation to gain a better understanding of key people and their business challenges. Successfully complete the new rebranding project for an existing product line. Meet with the CEO and gain feedback on what else I need to be working on to improve myself and to add further value to the organisation.

The main criterion for planning using short-, medium- and long-term goals is that you be flexible, prepared to change and adapt as circumstances and situations change. That is why it is critical that you review, revamp and reassess your goals regularly, adjust where you need to, change where required, and refocus on what is important and currently needed.

There is no right or wrong way; you need to find the best focus and approach for yourself. I have long-term goals to be completed two years from now. I have six-month milestones, then I focus my attention on the next 30 days and concentrate my efforts on what I need to do this week to move ever closer to my long-term goal.

This way I can adjust my course where required or as other opportunities arise that will get me closer to my long-term goal. With this type of thinking I can recognise and respond to new opportunities and not become locked into a mindset that this is the only way forward, as I have been guilty of in the past.

CHAPTER 17
Turning dreams into destinations

Think about how old you were five years ago. Have those years passed quickly? Where did the past five years go? Now add another five years to your age! Whether you have a goal or not, the next five years will go by just as quickly. The difference will be whether you end up where, or close to where, you want to be or nowhere in particular. This chapter is about setting your course and determining a destination you want to head towards.

From the previous chapter you now understand the connection between long-term, medium-term and short-term goals. So let's take it one step further, moving from macro (your lifetime dream list) to micro (the goals you would like to achieve in the next five years). In this chapter I would like to share with you the different areas in which you can create your long-term goals as you plan what you would like to achieve in the next five years.

There are six broad areas in which you can set your long-term goals ...

Family

What would you like to achieve as a family in the next five years? You may consider goals that have a positive impact on your immediate family members, your extended family or even friends that are like family to you. Just as companies need common goals to align the people and teams of the business, so do families.

I see families grow apart and people fall out of love, and I often wonder whether having a common goal or a shared vision might have averted that drifting apart. Most people start off a long-term relationship with a common interest or goal, and as the relationship progresses it is as though society sets the goals — move in together, buy a home, have kids, send them off to school, work hard, build a career, provide for your family. Then one day you wake up and think, 'What am I doing this for? What is life all about? Is this it for me?'

A number of families and couples have participated in our Passionate People Program. In some cases it is the first time in 20 years they have shared their dreams. It's not that people don't want to share; it's just that we all get busy being busy and life gets in the way of living. I am not saying that setting goals together as a family is a panacea for a great, long-lasting relationship or a loving, caring and together family, but it can't hurt.

So there are two questions you may want to consider as you think about what you want to achieve as a family in the next five years:

» What do you see yourself achieving as a family unit?

» In your family what milestones do you want to reach in the next five years?

Financial

The three things people stress about most are financial concerns, relationship challenges and health issues. Almost always stress comes from trying to control the uncontrollable, focusing on the worst-case scenario or giving up personal power to the issues rather than taking action on the solution to move yourself forward through the challenge. One way to combat the stresses that enter our lives is to put them into perspective, and the best way to do that is by having a vision of what is important to you and what matters to you.

So let's look at the financial goals you would like to achieve in the long term, five years from now. These are goals that relate to the financial milestones you would like to achieve, such as your level of personal or business debt, your income, the investments you have made to create a stronger financial position for you and your family, your bank savings or the funds you have created for your retirement. It is not just about money; it could be about the emotional security you feel when you are clear on where you are heading financially.

To clarify your financial milestones for the next five years, here are two questions to get the ball rolling:

» What do you see yourself achieving financially in your lifetime?

» What are the key financial milestones that you have accomplished?

Fitness

You have nothing if you don't have your health. This is about your health and fitness vision for the next five years. How fit and healthy do you need to be and want to be so you can do all the things you want to do? I am not a fitness guru or a gym junkie, but I do know that I am better for my family, for my business and for my audiences when I am fit and healthy. For me fitness equals energy, and I can do so much more and have a much bigger impact in the time allocated if I have plenty of energy.

It could be about losing excess kilos, attaining a certain level of fitness, slowing the biological clock compared with the calendar clock, overcoming an ailment or completing a physical challenge such as a marathon. There are a couple of questions you may want to ponder as you think about what you would like to achieve in this area of your life:

» Your health and fitness is the vehicle that carries you towards your vision, so how fit and healthy do you want to be in the next five years?

» What do you see yourself achieving personally in your health and fitness in the future?

Fun

Life is meant to be fun — not all the time but most of the time. When did you start taking yourself really serious and stop having fun? I get it that there are some times in your life when it is not fun: someone close to you passes away, a child is hurt, a tragedy affects your life. These things happen to us. They are part of the fabric of life. When and where we have fun needs to be woven in between and over the top of these not so great occurrences.

Now we all know that fun can happen naturally and spontaneously. However, there are some things we need to be more deliberate about as we look to the future. The first is determining what fun means to us and how we create it in our life. For me fun is created when I can unite my passions — my family or dear friends, my work, travel and photography. It doesn't have to be all of them happening at once, but it is a fun day when they do.

To give you an example, I was recently on a work trip in Wellington, New Zealand, where my family joined me. We arrived a day early and met up with a great friend of mine who is one of the best photographers in the world, Simon Woolf. Over the years he has taught me so much about photography. Simon gave me, Kristine and our two daughters a guided photography tour of his fair city and all of us took photos that day. It was a great day spent exploring and pursuing our passions, a fun family day.

So what do you need to think about when you set your long-term goals relating to fun?

» What activities, adventures and anticipated achievements will bring you joy and fun in the future?

» What do want to explore, achieve, pursue, create, discover, experience or participate in over the next five years that would be fun?

Meaningful

Life is too short to let it just slip by and not feel like you are making a difference to the people who matter to you. It is too short not to work on what's important to you, what matters and what is meaningful. For too long people have accepted that you do what is required to make a living and then when you retire or have time or have a few more choices, then you can do what you like. I am not talking about quitting your job or closing down your business. It is your responsibility to find the meaning and reason behind what you do with your time, energy and effort.

What is meaningful for me takes the shape of not only the work I do but also the contribution I make to others. It is how I earn a living and the knowledge I pass on to my children. It is the things I stand for, and not being afraid to stand up for what I believe in. It is what gives me joy, love and satisfaction. Four things I love to do are write, present, create and discover. Over the next five years you have a choice, it is either to create a recording that you were alive or create a life, just as an artist would create a great picture. My good friend and photography mentor, Simon Woolf, shared this quote with me from one of his own mentors Arthur Bates: 'Honesty in its intention is the difference between creating art and recording history.'

YOU ARE EITHER RECORDING HISTORY OR CREATING ART.

If you were to create a masterpiece titled 'My Life', what would you create?

» What type of career, work, roles or business do you want in order to feel your work contribution matters?

» What do you need to achieve to feel that what you do in either your personal or your professional life is meaningful?

Legacy

Everyone creates a legacy. Some are profound, positive and memorable for all the right reasons; others are memorable for all the wrong reasons. What type of legacy do you want to create for others to benefit from, that will live on after you have gone? How do you want to be remembered? It could be for a set of values or principles or beliefs that will have a positive impact on your children as they grow into adults. It could be for a set of skills or a knowledge bank that those who come in contact with you can use over and over again.

As Stephen Grellet's poem so eloquently states...

'I shall pass through this world but once. Any good. Therefore, that i can show to any human being. Let me do it now. Let me not defer or neglect it. For i shall not pass this way again.'

Over the next five years you are going to have an impact on the people around you. You can decide whether you make some deliberate choices about what impact you want to have on the people who mean the world to you, or whether you just take a chance and see what happens. If you want to be deliberate then consider these questions:

» What type of legacy do you want to create over the next five years?

» What do you want to be known for and your life to stand for? What living example do you want to offer those who matter to you?

The key is first to decide how you want to *feel* — this is how you obtain that emotional connection we have spoken about in previous chapters — and then follow this process...

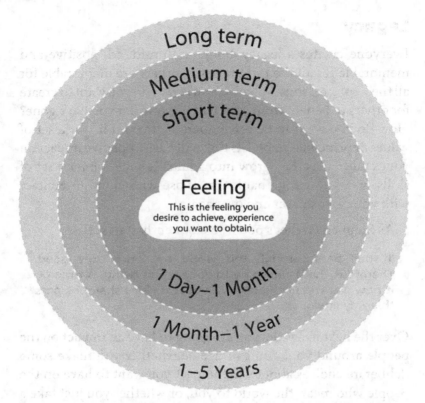

We have demographic gurus, statistical experts and actuarial boffins who can tell us how long we will live. That is nice to know, but if you want to know how much living will be done in your lifetime, you have to be your own predictor of that. It takes time to create great art, great achievements and great results. That is why it is vital to have a great vision.

CHAPTER 18
Creating the road map for the year ahead

David Starr Jordan, the founding president of Stanford University, was fond of sharing these words with his students: 'Wisdom is knowing what to do next, skill is knowing how to do it, and virtue is doing it!'

So what do you need to do next? Decide what you want to achieve, obtain, reach, have and become in the next 12 months. For most people the norm is wishing and hoping that their goals will come true, rather than knowing and planning for their goals to come true. The art of narrowing your focus to the next 12 months is taking your vision, those long-term goals, and turning them into achievable, believable and desirable goals.

Amat victoria curam is a Latin proverb first brought to my attention by my good friend and fellow speaker Malcolm McLeod. It translates as ...

'Victory loves preparation!'

This chapter is about being prepared to achieve those milestones that are vital for you to feel how you want to feel and that act as stepping stones to those long-term goals we spoke about in the previous chapter. It is about creating a series of dots that form an outline of a picture and then joining those dots together to make your picture come to life. Malcolm has another great saying: 'Unfocused thoughts equal unaccomplished results.' So I am going to ask you to become very focused on the following eight key areas, once again starting with your three driving emotions.

I'm often asked, 'How many goals should I set for the next 12 months and do I need one goal in each of the eight areas?' There are no rights or wrongs with this activity. You can have two or three goals in one area and none in another area. I only get concerned when people have six or seven of their goals in one area and none in any other area.

Family goals

As I mentioned in the last chapter, I am a great believer in setting goals as a family, whether they are activities you want to do together or characteristics you want to have as a family. It takes energy and effort to make families work well. This is one area that deserves an investment of your time, so take the time to have that meaningful conversation about what is important with the loved ones who mean the world to you.

» What would you like to achieve as a family in the next 12 months?

» What would you like to do for your family?

» What type of person are you going to become for your family?

» What are you going to achieve that your family will benefit from and enjoy?

Career/business goals

This can relate to the goals you want to achieve during your working life, whether as an employee or in your own business or in the small business you have on the side apart from your day job. It can relate to positions or roles you want to hold or achievements you want to be recognised for in your business. The milestones that are important to you could relate to a project you're working on, something you are creating or even securing that big deal.

» What would you like to achieve in your career or business?

» What type of roles do you want to be performing in your career?

» What would be a great job to do or business to own?

» What would you like to achieve in your business life?

Growth goals – personally and professionally

We are limited only by our ability to believe, our confidence to achieve and our imagination to dream what is possible. As you enhance your self-esteem, you also enhance your ability to believe in yourself and what you can achieve. What additional skills and knowledge do you want to obtain? What attitudes do you need to enhance? These goals could involve your going back to school or could be as simple as reading a book that will build your self-esteem and self-confidence to a new level. Or it could be making a conscious decision to network with more like-minded or positive people.

» What activities are you going to do in the next 12 months to develop your skills, knowledge and attitude?

» What courses are you going to attend to improve yourself?

» What do you need to achieve to become a better person?

» Who do you need to work with as a mentor to help you shift your thinking to the next level?

Financial goals

These goals are focused on the income you want to earn, the money you want to save or the investments you want to acquire. Think about what financial situations you want to change or have, or the results you want to obtain. It could be about reducing your debt. Review the goals you want to achieve in the long term, then ask yourself what goal you need to achieve in the next 12 months to carry you closer to your long-term goal.

» How much money do you want to earn in the next 12 months?

» How much do you want to save or invest?

» Which debts do you want to retire in the next 12 months?

» What personal financial circumstances do you want to change?

Fitness goals

This is an area that everything else revolves around. It's hard to achieve great things when you are not energised and healthy. These goals relate to recharging and re-energising your body, mind and spirit so you can feel you have enough for everyone and every situation, with energy to burn. These goals could be as simple as undergoing your annual medical check-up because it has been six years since you last had one, or completing your first 10-kilometre fun run, or shedding the surplus kilos you have put on over the past few years, or just exercising more consistently and regularly.

» How fit and healthy would you like to be in the next 12 months?

» What is your fitness goal for this year?

» What are some of the fitness activities you would like to pursue?

» How much more energy would you like to have in your life?

Community goals

You can contribute to your friends and your local community or even the international community in a number of different ways. You can donate your time, expertise, network, resources or money. Maybe your contribution is looking after the under 9s soccer team, organising a get-together dinner party with your close friends every quarter, welcoming a new neighbour to your street with a cup of coffee, or cleaning out your wardrobe and giving those surplus clothes to the local community store.

It could be an anonymous donation or travelling overseas to teach English to schoolchildren, or it could be sharing your business insights with school leavers. I know everyone is busy, but often the real beneficiary of giving is ultimately yourself. From my experience it is when I give or contribute that I am often given the greatest gifts or insights.

» What would you like to contribute to your community?

» What would you like to do for your friends in the next 12 months?

» What community activities would you like to be involved in?

» How do you contribute to others using your skills, time, knowledge, resources or expertise?

Lifestyle goals

This is about giving back to yourself. It is not necessarily about imitating the lifestyles of the rich and famous. I mentioned in a previous chapter that everyone has a 'battery' that needs to be recharged from time to time. Lifestyle goals give you back the energy to keep on doing what you want to do with vigour and vitality, whether it's taking time out to play sport or to pursue a passion. This energy comes from doing the things you love to do, making sure you have time for your passions. If you love to dance then dancing will give you back energy. It may take time but as a result you will always have more energy to do what is important.

» What are you going to do just for you?

» What rewards are you going to give yourself or your family?

» What are your passions and how often are you going pursue them?

» What goal would revitalise you, build your energy and recharge your batteries?

Adventure goals

Adventure could be about going parachuting or it could be about sitting on a white sandy beach sipping a cocktail on a relaxing island holiday. These goals are the places you want to visit, the things you want to see and do. They are the bigger goals that relate to your passions. If you're passionate about photography it could be attending a four-day *National Geographic* photography course in New York.

» What type of holiday would you like to take in the next 12 months?

» What type of adventurous activity would you like to do?

» Where would you like to travel and what would you like to do there?

» Which one of your destination goals from your list of 100 things are you going to complete in the next 12 months?

Decide on your deadline

Now a goal without a deadline is just a wish, so once you have written out your goals for the next 12 months you need to define when you want to achieve them by. Not every goal you write down is going to come true in 12 months: some will come true in the next 30 days, others in six months' time, and some you may want to coincide with your birthday. The key is to pick a day, a date, a month and a year. If you miss the deadline that's okay; reassess your goal and create a new deadline. Be realistic and create a sense of expectation. I often meditate or sit quietly to arrive at a feeling about whether the deadline I have set is realistic.

Then you need to remain focused on the goal, which as we have spoken about is always the hardest thing to do. Here is a useful template that you can download from www. passionatepeople.com, by scanning the QR code below or by using the Passionate People app; or you can purchase these cards to use when writing down your goals and then read them on a regular basis.

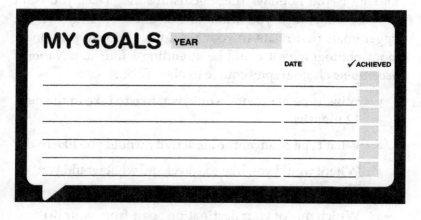

Thinking about everything we have talked about over the past two chapters, it can best be summed up this way: *Your vision is your compass and your goals are your map.* One assists you in finding your true north and the other plots the pathway towards it.

CHAPTER 19
Recognise, reflect, reset

What I have learned about goal setting and pursuing your passions is that you will be tested. The simple art of working towards your goal brings out your true character; it unveils the best in you, and the worst in you sometimes. You will be frustrated and delighted. You will pay a price; however, when you pursue something worthwhile, it is always an investment, not a cost. Some goals will be achieved more quickly than you anticipated, while others will take longer than you expected.

RECOGNISE YOU WILL BE TESTED.

Buddha himself thought ...

> 'What you are is what you have been. What you'll be is what you do now.'

What you do now is about working your plan, being tenacious when confronted with challenges and showing grit when those roadblocks are sent to test you. Understand that tenacity wins every race. I believe every challenge that is placed in front of us is sent to test our resolve.

The universe has a way of asking the question 'Are you serious about achieving this goal?' The road towards your goal will be filled with character-building opportunities that may very well be preparing you for a future challenge. As Albert Einstein said after many failed experiments, 'Adversity introduces a man to himself.'

Not everything will work out for you straightaway. What if you started a new enterprise and after months of planning, sourcing products, preparing displays and advertising, your business sales for the first day totalled $4.98? Would you be sufficiently focused and motivated to do it all again the next day?

The business I'm referring to here is Tiffany & Co. In 1837 Charles Lewis Tiffany and John B. Young opened their first store on Lower Broadway in New York City, and that was indeed their first day's take. Today Tiffany & Co. has more than 240 stores in 22 different countries and a turnover of $430 000 000. Everything starts off slowly. Success is not only about action; it's also about tenacity and the will to hold the course you have charted for yourself. The reason why most people give up is that success never comes first; it always follows action and belief.

REFLECT ON THE MESSAGES BEING GIVEN TO YOU

I often say...

'Everything is perfect!'

In testing times it is sometimes difficult to look for the reason, the message or insight, when you are in the middle of a disaster, but if you look at the set of circumstances then you can find the message, rather than living with the feeling of 'Why me and why now?'

Every decision you have ever made is perfect for that time, that place and that situation. It may not have been the right decision two hours, two days or even two years later but we don't live in the future. We plan for it of course, but we live in this day, right now.

So don't let the possibility of being wrong stop you. As one of my favourite authors, Seth Godin, said in one of his blog posts...

> 'The cost of being wrong is less than the cost of doing nothing.'

Reflect on what is working and what you have learned. Reflect on your successes, on the rewards and benefits and the remarkable things that have happened to you as you pursued the goal. Maybe they were the real gift, not the goal itself.

RESET YOUR GOALS

The Chinese mystic philosopher Lao Tzu once said...

> 'Great acts are made up of small deeds.'

As you pursue your goals remember that every goal is a series of small deeds or steps or actions done consistently within the timeframe you have set to achieve that goal. So take time to reset your goals, adjusting them from time to time if needed. A dear friend of mine once shared that she had had such a great year the previous year but that the first six months of this year were slow and unexciting; nothing was in flow. When I asked her what was great about the previous year she told me about all the goals she had achieved — promotion, new relationship, purchasing her first apartment and competing in her first triathlon. She had achieved a lot of the goals she had written down 12 months before in one of my workshops. Then I asked the question, 'Have you reset your goals for this year?' The light bulb went on and she began to create a new list of goals.

Take five minutes a week out of your schedule to review the progress you are making towards your goals, and refocus and reset your goals where needed. Then take 15 minutes once a month to plan the goals and actions for the following month. Once every 90 days take 30 minutes out to repeat the process, and then take a day out of your life to sit in a park, on your back deck, on the beach or somewhere in nature. This is your time for a personal treat: to think about the year ahead and plan out the goals you want to achieve in your life for the next 12 months.

CHAPTER 20
Letting go of expectations

Too often we focus our attention on actually achieving the goal, the end result, only to become frustrated by the slow progress we make. Think about the last time you went on a diet. You were focused, diligent and committed, you ate right, exercised right and you had the right discipline, but when you weighed yourself at the end of the week you felt like there was so much more to do. So you saddle up again for another perfect week — and the same result. You lose weight but never as much as you hoped for, so you become susceptible to doubt about the value of what you are doing.

As I explained in chapter 18, a goal can bring the best out in you but it can also be destructive, when people become obsessed with a goal to the point of needing it to happen so badly that it actually eludes them. If you worry too much about achieving the goal, you subconsciously send a message that you actually don't have confidence that it will come true. If you are confident, it *will* come true. Believe you are deserving of the goal and know you are capable of achieving it, then all you need do is take the appropriate action and let the universe manifest the right result for you.

The key to achieving your targets comes down to focusing on your goal (having it at the top of your mind) but not worrying about achieving it or giving it too much attention. Once you have set your goal and it's aligned to your driving values, let it go. Let go of your worry about whether or not it will come true. To do that, there are three focuses you need to have and they are all aligned to the *Feel — Think — Do* model, or your emotional, mental and physical connection.

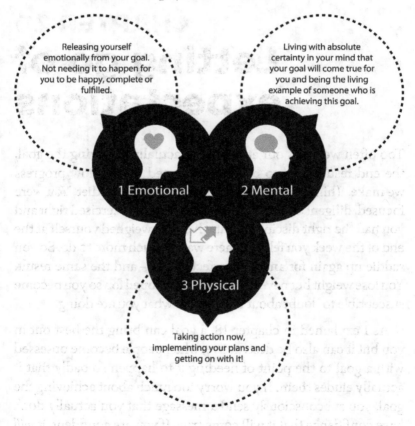

Releasing yourself emotionally from your goal. Not needing it to happen for you to be happy, complete or fulfilled.

Living with absolute certainty in your mind that your goal will come true for you and being the living example of someone who is achieving this goal.

1 Emotional

2 Mental

3 Physical

Taking action now, implementing your plans and getting on with it!

Emotional – releasing yourself

Release yourself emotionally from the goal itself. When you have an attitude that you actually don't need that goal to come in order to have a great life, to be happy or fulfilled, then the worry of whether or not it will come true vanishes, leaving you to channel that energy into taking action.

Focus on how you want to feel and turn your attention to the action you need to take. With the right mindset, when you let go of the pressure, expectations and worry, achieving your goals can become effortless. If there is one lesson I have learned that has benefited me the most over the past two years, it is this one: once I set a goal, I release it, which frees me to achieve the results I desire. As we spoke about in the previous chapter, there will be challenges, but when you know it is all part of the journey it makes sense.

Mental — living with certainty

A fun thing happens when you start living with more certainty: doubt is diminished, clarity forms, confidence grows and consistency becomes one of your normal personal traits. How do you act when you have certainty in your life? How would you act and feel now if you had absolute certainty? How would you respond to a challenge?

Most battles we face take place in our mind: Will they like me? What if it doesn't work? What will they think? Some people worry about the worst-case scenario, and that's okay if you have a balanced perspective and also consider the best-case scenario before deciding on the most likely outcome.

Physical — taking action

The only natural thing to do now that you are mentally and emotionally connected is to take action. Remember, activity cures inactivity. Nothing can replace action, not positive thinking or great confidence. By taking action you validate the mindset you have created and further strengthen and justify the belief you have in yourself. Every action you take adds another strand to the rope that is pulling you closer to who you want to be and what you want to achieve. When you take action you will always achieve a result. It will either move you closer to your goal or offer you a lesson that will help move you c loser to your goals in the future.

Part III
Mindset: gaining confidence in your life

CHAPTER 21
Who's stopping you?

In most cases it is not what is stopping you but *who* is stopping you, and that who is normally *you*! Circumstances and situations do play a part, but usually the root cause is you.

When we really get down to the roadblocks that stop people from pursuing their passion, taking advantage of their opportunities, tapping into their potential or achieving their possibilities, it is normally a conversation that starts with 'too'. You can fill in the rest—too hard, too busy, too tired, too long, too short, too much, too little, too easy, too many, too focused, too big, too small...

What is it for you? Think about a goal you want to achieve that you have repeatedly put off. What 'too' excuse are you using?

The way to get rid of the too from your life is to identify a bigger reason why, then forget about completing the goal and start focusing on taking the first step! Remember, the day you take the first step the task is 50 per cent completed. This relates directly to our self-belief, self-esteem and self-confidence.

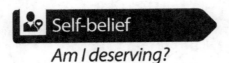

Am I deserving?

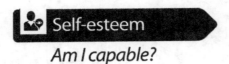

Am I capable?

Is it possible?

It comes down to the conversation you have with yourself when you set a goal or pursue a different path, and that conversation normally revolves around three questions that are connected to your self-belief, self-esteem and self-confidence ...

Am I worthy and deserving? Am I worthy of this success, the recognition I will receive from friends or family if I achieve the goal I have set myself? Do I deserve this result?

Am I capable? Do I have the skills, knowledge and abilities to achieve the goal? What if I try and fail — could I recover with some dignity? What else would I need to learn?

Is it possible? I know it is possible for other people to achieve that type of goal, but with my track record could I do so? Is it possible in the timeframe or would I need a superhuman effort to achieve it?

I don't know you personally of course, but the answer is *Yes*, *Yes* and *Yes*! Yes you can, but unfortunately my answer does not count.

You need to have a level of confidence that will see you to the point of starting. As I have said, it is not about finishing but about starting. You just need enough confidence to start taking action towards achieving the goal, because your confidence will grow when each of these actions and activities is completed.

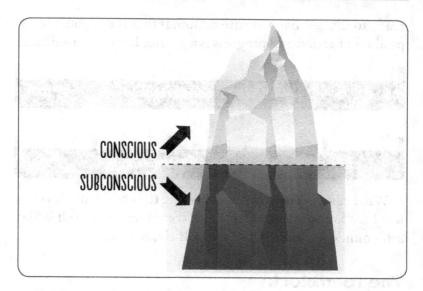

I like to use the analogy of the iceberg: it's what's under the surface that causes most damage, whether that's your subconscious, your beliefs or your level of confidence. How many people do you know who you believe have everything together, and yet when you really get to know them they have just as many doubts as you do? All of us have fears. It could be fear of failure, fear of success or fear of change. The only way to overcome your fear is through action. I love the quote ...

'if you face your lion on your pathway, it will disappear.'

When you take action, you face your fear. The more action you take, the more you build up your confidence. Each step, each time you do not give in to the temptation to stop, your confidence grows and your doubt diminishes.

So how much confidence do you need to get started? You may already be 100 per cent confident of reaching your goal, which means you have let go of your expectations and are ready to make it happen with action. If that is not you, the by-product of action and progress is a greater level of confidence.

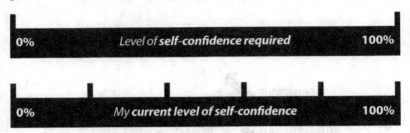

What can slow us down in achieving the confidence level we need are four roadblocks that can compromise our self-belief, self-confidence, self-esteem and self-awareness.

The roadblocks

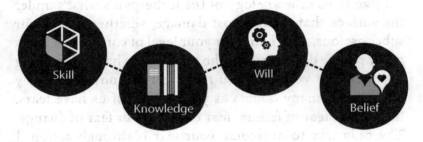

SKILL

To be the best you that you can be, you may need to improve or learn a set of different skills. They could be hard skills or soft skills and relate to either your personal or your professional development. For example, one of my goals is to take 1000 great photos around the world. I am 75 per cent confident I can do that, as I have already taken quite a few. (If you want to check some of them out, visit www.passionatepeople.com.) I know that for me to be able to achieve this goal, I am going to need to improve my skills, so I read magazines and books, and attend photography courses and retreats to learn the required skills.

KNOWLEDGE

To speed up the process of becoming 100 per cent confident, what additional knowledge do you need to achieve your goal? That knowledge may come from reading or being mentored by someone who is an expert in that field. Again, to give you an example focused on my professional field, one of my goals is to become a world-class presenter, and to do that I need a greater knowledge in how to tell compelling and engaging stories. So I have a great mentor I work with to enhance my knowledge of how to become better at my craft and of what works and what doesn't.

WILL

As I have mentioned more than once, tenacity wins every race. Your willpower, your willingness to start and to back yourself, is made up of your determination, drive and desire. It is your grit and resilience that determines your success. As the saying goes, 'You are not beaten if you don't stop.'

I love the quote on the dressing-room wall of the Manchester United Football Club...

'Determination separates people.'

It is your ability to stick at something when nothing seems to be happening on the surface, and underneath all that is going on are imperceptible gains. It is the willpower to plough on, to push through the doubt and to believe in yourself when no-one else will. *Tenacity wins every race!*

BELIEF

This is all about the challenge we spoke about at the start of this chapter — overcoming a belief that you are not worthy, not deserving, not capable, or that it is not possible for you to achieve it. Beliefs are formed from an early age through the people, situations and circumstances that we come in contact with during our lifetime.

All beliefs are 100 per cent right in your own mind, but they may not be true in reality. You probably know people who sometimes make outrageous statements that are clearly not true, but in their mind they are indisputable facts. However, you and I have not walked in that person's shoes, experienced what they have experienced and seen what they have seen. The challenge is when people who want to achieve a certain goal and have the skills and the knowledge to do so are held back by the roadblock of their belief system.

What is stopping you from being the best you that you can be? It could be a combination of all four roadblocks or only one roadblock that is the first domino you need to push over for you to be great. In the next chapter we will identify the specific areas that are holding you back from becoming an example of a person who is living with greater certainty every day.

CHAPTER 22
Your plate is only so big

We live in a fast-paced, busy-being-busy world where there is an endless to-do list, an ever-renewing set of deadlines and challenges that need our attention, and never enough time. I believe one of the key reasons people don't achieve their most important goals is as simple as that they have no space in their life, no energy to manifest and no room on their plate to allow that goal to come true.

To allow greatness to come into your life, you need to create space.

What do you need to let go of or stop doing? Sooner or later you need to let something go to free the space and time for your goals to manifest themselves in your life. The simple action of not doing something that holds you back sends a powerful message that you are willing to change and that a spot is open for what is important to you to come into your life.

It is hard to achieve all that you want when you have no time, no space and no energy. How are you going to do everything on your plate right now, let alone all the things you want to achieve in the future?

A common challenge some people face is a tendency to say yes to everything. All too often people with great potential and kind hearts suffer from yes-itis: Yes, I can do that for you. Yes, I am happy to help out. Yes, I have time to complete that project. Then when it comes to the crunch you are overcommitted and overwhelmed and wonder, 'How am I going to do all this?' When this happens you tend to put yourself last, and that situation can sometimes persist for years.

After almost two decades of working with people across the globe I have learned that everyone in their heart of hearts knows what they need to change.

ALL OF US KNOW IN OUR HEART OF HEARTS WHAT WE NEED TO START DOING IN OUR LIVES & WHAT WE NEED TO STOP DOING IN OUR LIVES.

Everyone knows what they need to change; the key is in creating the right environment or set of circumstances, introducing the most appropriate catalyst for that message to appear. To identify what you need to change in your life to become the best you that you can be, you need to ask yourself the right questions.

What do you need to let go of in your life? The easiest way to determine that is to ask yourself the following four questions. They are simple thought provokers and act as a sound catalyst to help you identify what you need to do now to achieve all that you are capable of achieving.

Think about the key areas of your personal life and your career or business life, then ask yourself...

Stop doing

What do you need to stop doing in your life in order for you to achieve all that you are capable of achieving? What is not serving you well? It could be a mindset, attitude, characteristic or activity that is slowing you down or holding you back from being the best you can be.

Maybe you need to stop:

» procrastinating

» putting yourself down

» doubting that you are good enough

» waiting for everything to be perfect before you start.

Start doing

What do you need to start doing if you are to achieve all that is possible for you to achieve? What have you been procrastinating over? What activity do you need to undertake that would bring out the best in you? What ritual, habit, behaviour or strategy, if you started it now, would propel you towards your goals so much more quickly?

Maybe you need to start:

» taking some action

» believing it is possible for you

» learning a new skill required to achieve your goal

» hanging out with people who will lift you up, not tear you down.

Do less

What do you need to do less of in your life? I am a realist; I get it that there are some things you cannot stop altogether, but you can do them less often. What consumes your time or mental energy? What do you have to slowly release from your life?

Maybe you need to do less:

» focusing on the negatives

» comparing yourself to others

» worrying about what others think about you

» second guessing whether this is the right thing to do.

Do more

What do you need to do more of in your life? There are some things you do that just work for you; the challenge is that you don't do them often enough. You are consistently inconsistent. You start it and it works and then you become distracted, lose focus — and you wonder why you don't do it more often.

Maybe you need to do more of the following:

» taking risks

» having fun, laughing and enjoying yourself

» finding reasons to do it and why it will work

» telling people you love them and are grateful they are in your life.

Sometimes we don't need more answers, we just need to ask more questions. Whether on a conscious or a subconscious level, you know what you need to do to move forward. You just need to have the courage and confidence to listen to the answer and then act on it. You just need to get out of your comfort zone and do what may be uncomfortable or inconvenient.

THE ANSWERS ARE ALWAYS IN THE QUESTIONS YOU ASK YOURSELF.

The questions on the previous pages are about bringing to the forefront what you know and being brutally honest with yourself. As the Ethiopian proverb so eloquently states, 'He who conceals his disease cannot expect to be cured.'

Any condition that stops you being the best you that you can be in your life, for your family, for your friends, for your colleagues and for the community you live, work and play in, is something that needs an antidote.

CHAPTER 23
Real education is igniting what's inside you

I believe you need to *grow there mentally before you go there physically*. You need to acquire the success mindset first before you can achieve your goals in reality. To achieve all that you are capable of achieving, you need to gain the level of belief, skill and knowledge that is required to obtain and maintain that success. In other words, you need to grow mentally into the person you need to be to achieve the goal you desire.

It is the process of developing the belief, skill and knowledge needed that creates a mindset that turns your potential into a world of possibilities that will sometimes take you to places beyond your wildest imagination. When you are mentally prepared you start to change your physical state, how you walk, talk and present yourself to others, which in turn starts the manifestation of those goals that are most important to you. To put it another way, prior planning prevents poor performance.

So what do you need to do to become the living example of the person who is achieving all that you are capable of?

In the previous chapter you identified what you need to stop doing, start doing, do less of and do more of in your life. Now let's look at how you can move to the next level. Below are the eight areas you can focus on to personally and professionally develop yourself...

Over the next couple of chapters we'll look at some of the options you have for your own personal development.

Tom Peters famously said...

'if you don't add something to your resume every year you are obsolete.'

He was not talking about changing jobs or careers, but about the act of continuously adding and refreshing your skills and knowledge to keep ahead of the career curve or life curve, the ability to change before you need to or are made to change, to keep growing and evolving as you go through life.

Learning

You and I cannot afford to stop learning, yet most people stopped learning when they left school or university. They had completed that learning process, which they saw simply as a means of acquiring a certain status, job or title. Or they just survived the ordeal of higher or tertiary education. The people who achieve the most are the people who become lifelong learners. They learn because they want to, not because they have to. They see the benefit and connection in learning both personally and professionally. Learning to live a better life and to become better as a person is as important as living itself.

The key to learning is to put yourself in inspiring learning environments on a regular basis. These could be courses, programs, workshops or seminars that relate to your career development or your hobbies, interests or a particular skill or area in your life you want to work on, or just think would be fun to do. For myself, I want to place myself as a student in a learning environment every quarter. The best place to start is to *define* what you want to learn, then *decide* what is the best way to learn that skill or gain that knowledge, and then *design* a plan of action that best suits your needs and circumstances.

There are so many learning options these days, from courses of different lengths to online webinars or face-to-face programs to following blog posts. Over the past couple of years I have put myself in all types of learning environments, from photography retreats to presentation skills programs to creativity conferences, and the amazing aspect is that I have always walked away with new knowledge or a new skill that has assisted me in another part of my life not directly related to this learning experience.

These chapters are about what you can do to *exercise your brain*. Scientific research tells us that physical exercise and learning increases the neurogenesis of our brain—in other words, as we learn and exercise we create new neurons. As we all know, if we are active mentally and physically we live longer and lead more productive lives.

So what are you doing to build up your mental muscle this year? No-one wants to get old before their time, and no one wants to lose their capacity to think better. Just as your car needs a service from time to time, your brain needs a maintenance plan.

In the next couple of chapters we will explore a number of other ways for you to learn, create, design, investigate or experience what is going to strengthen your mental muscle this year and in the years ahead.

CHAPTER 24
Fill your mind with transforming information

We all have a choice when it comes to what influences us. What we listen to on a regular basis influences our thinking; who we allow near our mind shapes how we act and respond. My first exposure to the world of personal growth was through books, seminars and audio tapes.

I turned off the radio in my car and started to listen to motivational and informational speakers. My thinking started to move from *I don't know if I can achieve that* to *I think I can achieve it* to *I know I can achieve it!* Like everything it is a process, one that involves sometimes flushing out the negatives and replacing them with positive information, possibility thinking and passionate success stories.

I rarely listen to the car radio now, but I do listen to podcasts, audiobooks, workshop audio content, and interviews with people whom I respect and who inspire me. So listening is the next way to develop yourself.

The great thing about listening to content is that you can be doing a couple of things at once — driving the car and listening to a podcast, going for a walk and listening to an audiobook, cooking dinner and listening to an audio recording. Your subconscious absorbs the information and files it away for a later day. So turn your down time into a time to shape your mindset and increase your knowledge.

Included in this category of learning is YouTube. Watching someone demonstrate a process or procedure is a great way to absorb information and learn new skills. Recently I was struggling to master some video editing software when my youngest daughter, who was 12 at the time, came to my rescue. Seeing my frustration she gave me an insight I hadn't considered: 'Just YouTube it, Dad — you can learn anything from there.'

Never before has there been so much no-cost or low-cost information available that we can listen to and watch on a range of electronic devices from smartphones to computers to e-readers or tablets, 24/7. We have access to some of the best minds in the world, leading authorities in anything you want to learn, whose wisdom and knowledge can be delivered to the palm of your hand.

You can access podcasts on iTunes, university lectures on iTunesU, audiobooks from www.audible.com, online recordings for some of the best speakers, lecturers, professors and other authorities in the world. There is no excuse that you can't access the information you desire to learn.

My suggestion is that you begin by *searching* for the podcasts that relate to what you want to learn, *start* listening to them and then *summarise* the key messages so you can reflect on them later or implement their ideas now. I like to listen to podcasts and audio recordings in my car, when I am at the gym or when I exercise outdoors. I know other people turn off the TV and use an hour of that time becoming better, learning more and improving their knowledge, an hour each day.

There is no crime in paying for audio programs from people you respect, admire and resonate with who you believe can assist you in your journey. A funny thing happens when you invest in yourself: you are more inclined to use the content, listen to the audio programs and reuse them over and over again.

I love this quote ...

'The grass is not greener on the other side of the fence — it's greener where you water it.'

The water is filling your mind with transforming information. The grass can be greener where you are — you just have to water it.

CHAPTER 25

The power of positive association

Genchi genbutsu (pronounced *gen-g gam-but-sue*) is a Japanese expression meaning 'Go and see' or 'Go to the source'. Whenever you or I think about changing, taking a different path or pursuing our passion as an enterprise, we should be prepared to go and see how others are doing it.

We need to be humble enough to 'sit at the feet of a master' — to watch and learn. Too often we bounce our passionate idea off friends or family members who have little or no expertise in the area of endeavour we want to pursue and so are not in a position to offer qualified advice.

Networking

The first port of call should be to talk to or study someone who is walking a path you want to pursue. Associate with people who are on a journey similar to your own. It is always difficult to explain what you are passionate about, whether it is photography or writing or painting or volunteering overseas, to someone who has never walked that journey. That is why it is critical for you to go to the source and gain insights, inspiration and information from those who you connect to the passion you are pursuing.

The power of positive influence is increased when you mix with people who share your interest or connection, those who are travelling a similar journey. Whether they are ahead of you or behind you on the journey, sharing and learning from these people is profoundly transforming. Take every opportunity to mix with like-minded people and to seek out those who are doing what you want to do, who have walked the path you want to pursue.

You have many choices in how you network with others. There are online communities, structured networks and organisations, or informal associations such as mastermind groups. There is an association, organisation or community group for just about anything you will be interested in that you can join to gain access to people who have the knowledge you seek.

ASSOCIATIONS

Look for those associations that relate to your passions or hobbies, or industry groups that relate to your career. To find out the best association for you, research which ones your peers or colleagues have links with. The great thing about associations is that most people involved are happy to share, help or offer encouragement. Go online and do your research.

ONLINE COMMUNITIES

There are many discussion groups, forums and communities whose conversation you can join as a follower, a contributor or a facilitator. Google your areas of interest and opt into some of these conversations. Consider putting out a Google Alert so you can track the topics and areas that appeal to you. I have made some great connections with people through responding to a blog or commenting on their website. Join in the conversation; you never know where it may lead you.

INFORMAL NETWORKING

On a number of occasions I have created my own group of like-minded people. I currently belong to an informal group of professional speakers, and we get together once every six months for three hours for lunch or coffee and indoor cricket. We share what has been working, what has not worked, what trends we see happening, and then a lot of fun and laughter. We never have an agenda and whoever can attend does.

MASTERMIND GROUPS

A more structured, purposeful networking opportunity can be to create your own group and invite a group of like-minded people to meet regularly to share ideas, insights and information within a mastermind group. One person I have been fortunate enough to know and to work with is Sarina Eggers, who once a month would organise a group of her women friends to catch up and share their goals and progress. Everyone became accountable to each other. They celebrated their successes together and encouraged each other to take the next step.

The best approach is to A.S.K. — Ask, Seek and Know. *Ask* questions of people who are doing and achieving what you want to achieve. *Seek* answers from those people or resources. *Know* how best you can apply this knowledge to your own situation.

−A.S.K.−
ASK; SEEK; KNOW. ASK QUESTIONS,
SEEK A RESPONSE, KNOW
HOW TO APPLY THE INFORMATION.

CHAPTER 26
Create time & space to think

I believe that every day we gain ideas, insights and information that can make a difference. These ideas may not be useful right away, but they may be further down the track. Being able to capture your thoughts and access them later is an asset whose value most people don't fully grasp.

Journaling

You have a number of choices when it comes to capturing your insights and ideas. You can buy yourself a notebook from the stationery store, set up an electronic document on your chosen device or even download a voice recording app to your smartphone. I recommend placing a number of notepads where you often have great ideas — beside the bed, on your office desk, in the kitchen and in your car.

In 2012 I attended the Behance 99% Conference in New York, where Harvard professor and co-author of *The Progress Principle* Teresa Amabile spoke about the value of keeping a daily journal. She had conducted an analysis of 12 000 journal entries from 238 senior executives from 26 different project teams, seven companies and three industries across the USA. She asked them to keep a journal every day as a way of reflecting on the day, refocusing them for the next day, capturing the ideas gained, celebrating the wins and what they had learned.

I am a great believer in journaling, and Teresa offered some great ideas to help start the process:

» Start small, setting aside five minutes a day.

» Decide on your medium — for example, a paper journal or an electronic app.

» Write, sketch or doodle.

» Use a set time of the day and set a reminder on your phone.

» Record progress, setbacks, horrors, hassles, challenges, celebrations, confidence boosters and crystal-clear moments.

» Write about whatever you like, but write *every day for 30 days*!

I have a very good friend and colleague who uses her smartphone every day to note what she is grateful for and what she has learned from the day.

Journaling, then, can take many forms — pick the one that best suits you.

Reflecting

Most people don't do enough of this. The key here is to take time out of our busy daily life to stop and reflect on what is working and what is not, and to decide what to do about it. Reflecting is also about being still, quieting the mind in order to listen to your intuition, to meditate and relax.

All too often we are so busy being busy that we never truly relax, slow down or are still for long enough to review our progress, correct a course and adjust our direction. Do you ever feel like you are travelling through life so fast that you just don't know where time goes, what you have achieved in the past week or where the year has gone? Through reflection we can allow life to catch up with us.

There are a number of different approaches you can choose from to use the process of reflection effectively. You can allocate a time each day to meditate, sit in a quiet place, focus on your breathing and be still. Meditation is a discipline that requires patience and practice. It is useful to take an introductory course on it or at least to download a guided meditation audio recording to assist you. Just start off small, taking five minutes out of your day, and work up to 15 minutes. Understand this simple fact: 1 per cent of every day is almost 15 minutes. Don't you deserve to take 15 minutes off to just focus on you?

Another option is simply to set aside five minutes each day to review, reflect and refocus. Review what is working and what isn't, and any adjustments you need to make. If you really believe in working on yourself, then I encourage you to take out 15 minutes a week to reflect on the past week, review what you need to improve on for next year and refocus on the goals you want to achieve next week.

Research tells us that each of us has approximately 70 000 thoughts per day. How many of yours:

» lift you up?

» tell you it is possible?

» give you the confidence to step outside your comfort zone?

» encourage you to pursue a new goal or passion?

» tell you to take the next step?

Shouldn't one of your top priorities be to control and channel your thoughts at least once a day?

To take this concept to the next level, allocate an hour a month, two hours a quarter, half a day every six months and a day a year to working on yourself, defining your goals, working on your plans, realigning your purpose and refocusing on what is important, what matters and what is going to make a difference. This is your own personal self-development retreat.

Bill Gates calls them Think Weeks. A couple of times a year he would spend time by himself and just think about his business, life and family, about what was next, what was around the corner and what was beyond.

From time to time each of us needs to become an Impartial Spectator — someone who can stand outside of ourselves to watch the person within behave, think, react and take action. When you can step outside to observe yourself doing the things you enjoy, the things that frustrate you and the things you need to change, you gain a perspective that can carry you to another level in your life.

Be a spectator of yourself and note where you can improve, the areas you have mastered and the action steps you need to take next time to gain better results. Remember...

**IT IS NOT ABOUT BEING THE BEST,
IT IS ABOUT BECOMING BETTER.**

Sabbatical

It is built into our DNA to want every goal now, fully knowing that there is a process and a series of steps to achieving it.

The Japanese have a proverb, *Ishi no ue ni mo sannen*, which literally means: 'Three years upon a stone'. Too often we don't have enough patience and perseverance in our pursuit of our passions, goals and desires. In so many cases the act of pursuing our goals has benefits beyond the goal itself; it leads us to discover who we are, who we are not and who we want to be. You may not have to sit on a rock for three years. I have given myself permission to stop and reflect by having an extended break from the work I do, like a sabbatical.

All too often when we become tired or bored with what we are doing, it is not about changing our role or job. It is just about falling in love with what we are doing again. There have been times in my speaking career when I just was not in love with what I was doing. So I took an extended break for two months, freshened up my thinking and fell back in love with my work.

Go and sit on the rock and reflect on what is important to you.

CHAPTER 27
Readers are leaders!

The prolific and wonderful author John Maxwell once said: 'Readers are Leaders'. I believe if you want to lead your life, you need to read books that inspire, inform and offer insights — then you can start to truly lead yourself. The first personal development book I ever read was *How to Win Friends and Influence People* by Dale Carnegie. That book was a great catalyst for me, making me aware of what I needed to do to get along with people.

I was never a great reader at school, yet today I am reading more than ever before. I have a thirst for knowledge because I know that I have found great answers, wonderful solutions and transformational strategies in books. In other words, I have found a better version of myself in the books I have read. I have found strengths that I possess, weaknesses I need to work on and answers to questions that have perplexed me. I have also read books I thought were terrible, only to read them again two years later to think they were fantastic.

Through research we know that the average person reads less than one book a year. Maybe that could be why many of them are living an average life, with average results. The best minds

I know are people who read a lot; they consume knowledge and let their mind be stretched.

Three options are to buy a print book, download a book onto an e-reader such as a Kindle or iPad, or listen to an audiobook from www.audible.com. Visit www.passionatepeople.com to access my recommended reading list.

I have a couple of different ways I go about selecting the right book for me. The first is I like to go to bookstores and see what book jumps out at me, whether it is an inspirational biography, an instructional 'how to' book or an informational trendsetter. I browse online for books that are similar to ones I have read or are recommended by people who purchased the earlier books. Finally, and I know this may sound funny, but if three different people recommend the same book to me I take it as a sign, and nine times out of ten I find it is the right book at the right time for me.

With great insights come great results. If you want to live a bigger life, then you need to think bigger about what is possible for you. Reading can transport you to what is possible for you. It gives you the hope and the *how* to become better, do better and be better.

Hazel Rochman writes about reading...

'Reading takes us away from home, but more importantly, it finds homes for us everywhere.'

Understand that sometimes you may only read a book for one chapter or for a single quote. It may contain just the message you need to hear today in the set of circumstances you are experiencing right now.

The usual pushback I get when I recommend reading is from people who say to me, 'I'm not a very good or fast reader.' That's okay. What is better — reading one page a day or zero pages a day? It's not about how fast you read or if you fall asleep while you read; the most important thing is that you start to consume content that will shape and influence your mindset now and that will have an impact on your life in the future. It's never too late to start.

CHAPTER 28
Sit at the feet of a master

I have always been a great believer in having coaches and mentors in my life. People you trust to tell you the truth, to guide you when you need it, to encourage you when you are on the right track and even to give you a push when you are procrastinating over something in your life. I have had great sporting coaches, great business coaches, great fitness coaches and great presentation skills coaches. I have always looked for mentors to bounce ideas off, to learn from and to watch as they have transitioned themselves in their career or business.

Often when the subject of coaches and mentors is raised people argue that they know what they need to do and they don't need any more answers or ideas. This may be true but you do need to be accountable to someone, and that's where a coach can play a critical role. For myself, I know I thrive when I have a coach. When I think I have all the answers, that's when I know I am on the slippery slope of decline.

I am not the only one who believes in the power of having a coach. Over the years I have worked with and had the chance to interview a number of CEOs of large companies; very few of them don't use a coach or mentor.

When I facilitated a panel of CEOs for a Toyota Dealer Conference in Perth, Australia, the panel included Managing Director of Wesfarmers Corporation, Richard Goyder, AO. Wesfarmers owns Coles, Target, Officeworks and Bunnings, as well as coal-mining, insurance, chemicals, energy and fertiliser companies. At the time of writing the company was valued at $40 billion. I asked the question, 'What do you do as part of your personal and professional growth?' His reply was simple: 'I have a business coach based in Queensland I meet face to face or on the phone once a month.' That was a turning point for me. If the MD of a successful multibillion-dollar business has a coach, why wouldn't I have one?

THE BEST GET BETTER NOT BY THINKING THEY HAVE ARRIVED BUT BY CONTINUING TO GROW.

There are two questions I am commonly asked about coaches: How do you find a coach, and what is the difference between a coach and a mentor? First, the difference between a coach and a mentor is simple: a mentor is someone you admire, follow or connect with informally. You may know them personally and meet with them from time to time, or you may just consume all of their information and follow their ideas.

A coach, on the other hand, is someone you have engaged or arranged to work with on a regular, structured basis. This could be a service you pay a fee for or a regular meeting you organise with a colleague who is coaching you and you pick up the lunch bill.

How do you find a coach? Look for people who inspire you, inform you and give you insights. Connect with them through email and see if they are willing to have a coffee or spend some time on the phone catching up with you about what they have learned through their career or business that they would be happy to share with you.

The worst thing that could happen is they say they don't have the time. But a funny thing happens: leaders *find* time and are often happy to share their insights on a regular basis. This approach has worked for me when seeking a mentor.

THE ANSWER IS NO, IF YOU DON'T ASK.

When I invest in a coach to work with me I look for people who are further along the journey than I am. I seek opinions from people I respect about who they believe are authentic leaders in that particular field, then I read their content and log onto their blog to see if their philosophy and my values are aligned.

Take the time to share your dreams with others. Achievement is never an individual activity. We all need support, and this will only happen when we share our plans and visions. You may need just a comforting word, a little push or some additional motivation to take you that extra mile.

Napoleon Hill, author of the all-time classics *Think and Grow Rich, The Law of Success* and *Success through a Positive Mental Attitude*, once said ...

'When two minds come together, a third mind is created.'

Don't try to do it all by yourself — use the power of synergy by working with a coach or mentor.

CHAPTER 29

There is no substitute for experience

We can talk about it, think about it and philosophise about it, but to truly gain a sense of whether it is the right job, hobby or business for you, there is nothing like going out and doing it. Experiencing is about taking yourself out of your known environment and trying something different or new.

It could be learning something outside your normal area of interest or expertise. Over the past couple of years I have engaged in very different types of learning experiences for no other reason than to gain a different perspective. I'm fortunate in that I have been able to look inside a Toyota car manufacturing plant in Japan and learn the value of continuous improvement. I've attended a photography retreat in New York, where Bob Sacha from *National Geographic* taught me the value of being curious and looking for what is around the corner. I've attended a Buddhist meditation course to realise the value of being still and listening to my intuition.

It is this willingness to engage in different experiences with an open mind and an open heart that I believe helps us to hear those messages that will shape our thinking in the future. The next level of experiencing is taking the time to pursue an interest, to try something new just once.

My eldest daughter wanted to take up archery as a sport. She did her research and organised the date to attend the introduction session. She was excited: 'I really want to do archery,' she told me during the days and weeks leading up to it. After that first session she never wanted to do it again. That's okay. It's about going out and experiencing it to see if it is right for you.

Over the years that I have run my Passionate People Program I have had numerous conversations with people about what they would love to do during their lifetime. People tell me about their perfect job or business, and you can see their desire to pursue that passion. I often ask, 'Have you ever worked in that role or business before?' Eight times out of ten they say no.

My thinking is if you want to be a florist, before you pursue that career or buy into that business, approach your local florist and ask them if you can come in on a Saturday and work for them for free. Go and spend a day working with a franchisee and gain an insider's view of what they do and how they do it.

Ask if you can be the bag carrier or shadow of the best salesperson or manager in your company, and see what makes them the best. It's not always obvious why they are the best, but if you hang around them you soon start to see the little things they do that make all the difference.

SUCCESSFUL PEOPLE LEAVE CLUES.

On any number of occasions I have had people say they would love to become a professional speaker and I have invited them to travel with me to a presentation to see what it's like behind the scenes. You will find that people are happy to help. They will rarely consider you a threat or imagine you are going to steal all their best ideas. Most very successful people are secure and happy to share. They have an abundant mentality because they started out where you are starting.

Now more than ever if you want to study a particular subject or for a particular degree, educational institutions will offer an introductory session, open day, short course or weekend workshop that will help you discover whether it is really what you want to do. You can also gain valuable insights by talking to students who have done or are doing the course.

Another idea is to create your own 'study tour' by approaching five businesses you admire and asking for a guided tour. The greatest gift I have been given as a professional speaker, consultant and facilitator is the opportunity to look inside businesses to see how they tick. You can see how businesses have become successful, observe their culture in action and the ideas that give them a competitive edge, and then determine how you can apply these ideas to your own life or role or business.

Over the next six months pick something new you want to experience — a hobby or interest or a new career. Then do your research and test it, even if it is just once. This one activity will be a catalyst that will either fuel your passion or clarify that it is not for you. We become too insular in our lives. Step out of your comfort zone and experience what other businesses, roles and learning environments have to offer.

One of the most extraordinary back stories of the 2012 London Olympics was the tale of Ugandan runner Stephen Kiprotich, who won the gold medal in the men's marathon. What is fascinating is that he took up marathon running only in 2011, and then only by chance!

He was asked to be a pace runner for the Ugandan marathon runners in training. His job was to run ahead of the group at a fast pace and drop off at the halfway point, where another runner would take over as pace runner. Only Stephen decided to keep on running for fun. He won the marathon and decided to train full time. In the post-race interview Kiprotich, aged 23, who had never been on the podium of a major marathon, said, 'Now, I am known and I am happy that I am known.'

Until you go and experience different activities, how do you truly know what hidden and unique talent you may have and may even become known for?

CHAPTER 30
You are a great investment

I'm not sure if there is such a thing as mental malnutrition, but I do see a lot of people who walk around in a trance, zombie-like, starved of professional or personal growth. They go through their day-to-day roles without any real energy.

If food gives us fuel then personal growth activity gives us hope and confidence. It gives us greater belief in our abilities, the capacity to be better, do better and achieve better results. When was the last time you sat down to a feast of personal growth and development material? Which book are you currently reading? What learning environment are you going to engage with in the next 90 days?

There are no calories in personal and professional food so go ahead and consume as much as you like. You should become the number one investor in your own dreams and development. I love the quote ...

'If you don't invest in yourself, you are a poor judge of a good investment.'

What does that mean to you? You need to invest time, energy, effort and money in yourself. Yes, even money. What is it worth to you to achieve your goals and dreams more quickly or with less effort by working smarter?

I have many opportunities to chat with people about their goals, passions and dreams, and I can always tell how committed they are by what they are willing to invest in *right now* to pursue their goals. Your investment could be taking the time to research online to discover what is available, putting the energy into taking action, making the effort to learn a new skill, enrolling in a workshop or seeking out knowledge from people who have walked the path before you on the journey you want to take.

Here are some ideas from previous chapters summarised for your review. The first step is to pick the opportunities that appeal most to you ...

☐ Enrol in a short course at a community college.

☐ Study for a university degree.

☐ Go on weekend retreats.

☐ Sign up for one-day programs.

☐ Attend a half-day workshop.

☐ Enrol in a series of evening courses.

☐ Explore company development programs.

☐ Participate in webinars.

☐ Listen to podcasts.

☐ Watch web TV shows.

☐ Watch YouTube educational videos.

☐ Enrol in iTunesU.

☐ Send out Google Alerts.

- ☐ Subscribe to blogs.
- ☐ Listen to digital audio recordings.
- ☐ Join or start networking groups.
- ☐ Join associations and community-based organisations.
- ☐ Join online communities and forums.
- ☐ Create your own group of like-minded people — a mastermind group.
- ☐ Buy a paper journal.
- ☐ Download a voice recording app for your smartphone.
- ☐ Create a digital ideas document on your electronic device.
- ☐ Buy a book — digital or paper version.
- ☐ Use a digital e-reader app or device.
- ☐ Read book abstracts (short 4 to 10 page summaries) of recommended books.
- ☐ Be still for 15 minutes a day.
- ☐ Learn to meditate.
- ☐ Create a weekly, monthly, quarterly, half yearly and annual refocus retreat.
- ☐ Take a sabbatical from what you do.
- ☐ Find a mentor and learn from their experiences.
- ☐ Invest in a coach to work with you.
- ☐ Create your own study tour.
- ☐ Go and experience the role you desire before you commit to it.
- ☐ Volunteer to work for free in the type of business you desire to create.

John Wooden, the great basketball coach, when asked about his regular daily routine, responded simply ...

'I worked on me being a better me! ... so what do you work on each day in your life?'

I know we all have to-do lists, project lists, shopping lists, must-do lists, have-to lists and should-do lists. I want you to create a YOU list.

Choose ideas you could explore for your own personal and professional development. Create a three-month personal and professional list — your growth plan. This is where you record what action you are going to take each week over the next three months to improve yourself. It could look something like this ...

FIRST MONTH

Week 1
Complete my online research about which courses I can do

Week 2
Start reading Linchpin *by Seth Godin*

Week 3
Call Paula Jones to see if we can meet for coffee to discuss mentoring

Week 4
Start being still for 15 minutes a day

SECOND MONTH

Week 1
Speak to HR about what development programs are available at work

Week 2
Download three podcasts to listen to this week

Week 3
Have my next meeting with my new mentor—share my growth plan

Week 4
Spend an hour reviewing my goals and planning the next month

THIRD MONTH

Week 1
Keep a journal for the month each day

Week 2
Start my six-week community college course on photography

Week 3
Have my next meeting with my mentor—discuss my 60 day progress

Week 4
Start my company effective communication skills program

I meet some amazing people as I travel the world, but one person stands out for me as a lifelong learner — Bob Roth. I met Bob in 2012 at a *National Geographic* photography retreat in New York. Bob and I share the same passion for photography and love for learning. We became friends and met up again later in 2012 in his home state of California, where he took me and an Australian mate of mine based in California flying in his light aircraft for the day. Bob has had six different legal careers, including specialising in commercial law, property law and criminal law. He learned how to fly a plane in his retirement. He is a keen pro-am photographer and scuba diver, a grandfather, married more than 45 years, and at the tender age of 73 is still taking courses at UCLA.

Invest in yourself and you will reap the rewards throughout your life.

Part IV
Momentum: living consistently in your life

CHAPTER 31

It's not about motivation, it's about creating momentum

The only person who can motivate you is you! People can inspire you, inform you and assist you in gaining better insights, but *you* need to take action. Move yourself from having great intentions to implementing them. Over the next few chapters we are going to focus on what it means to create momentum in your life.

As an analogy, think of two trains — one stationary and the other moving. At the end of every train line is a buffer stop consisting of a reinforced timber brace that prevents a stationary train from running off the end of the track. Now if that train was travelling at 100 kilometres an hour, five metres of reinforced concrete would not stop it. What's the difference? One has momentum — it is not thinking about getting started! It's moving ahead — fast!

To achieve all you deserve, desire and are determined to achieve in your life, you need to create momentum. It's about taking action, getting into flow and pushing through any resistance or reservations you may be experiencing.

At the beginning of this book we spoke about the big picture and your long-term vision. Now we are going to move from macro to micro, to focus on the micro actions you can take to move from where you are now to where you want to be.

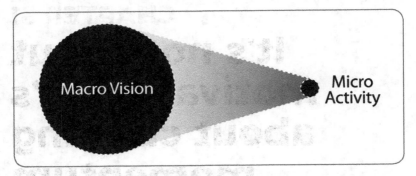

There are four key factors involved in creating the momentum we need to propel us towards our goals and desired outcomes.

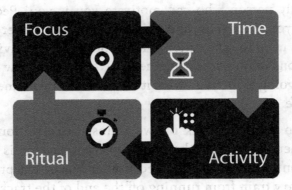

Focus

The easy part is setting the goal; the hardest is staying focused on it. People who achieve the most in the shortest time are focused. They focus on the activities that count and they don't get distracted by challenges or setbacks or the noise around them.

This observation by British writer Stuart Wilde really struck a chord with me ...

'Opportunities move towards order, balance & power. They move away from scattered over-energised people & flee at high speeds from confusion & lack of consistency.'

In other words, when you know what you want and why you want it and are focused, the right opportunities are clear to you. So often people get excited about opportunities and possibilities but fail to give them the necessary focus and consistency, and then wonder why it just doesn't happen for them.

Time

Make the most of your time. You need to shift your thinking from managing tasks that take up your time to managing the priorities in your life to gain the most from your time. Each of us has 24 hours a day to spend however we choose to. It is one of the few aspects of life that is consistent for everyone. It is also the one thing that can separate the people who achieve from those who just get by, existing but never really living.

People become frustrated when they don't make progress, yet if they never allocate the time to make progress towards their goals, then how do they expect to achieve them? The Buddhists have a saying ...

'You don't have as much time as you think.'

We tend to overestimate how much we can achieve in a year and underestimate what we can achieve in our lifetime. The key is to keep on persisting.

What if you have a dream to become an author to provide for your family, but you live in a tiny flat that is infested with mice, you are on welfare to support your only daughter and at least 27 publishers have said your book is not good enough to publish? What do you do? Give up, get a job, be satisfied with just getting by, or give it another go? J.K. Rowling's *Harry Potter* books went on to sell more than 400 million copies and gross over $7.7 billion. In less than 10 years she became one of the wealthiest women in the world.

Activity

At the end of the day nothing happens until someone acts. It is never about your intentions. Everyone has good intentions. It's about taking action that gets you closer to where you want to be. For J.K. Rowling it was writing in the evenings when her daughter went to bed, rather than watching TV, and it was knocking on one more publisher's door after the first 27 had turned her down.

I know this sounds simplistic, but *activity cures inactivity*. Get yourself moving. Maybe it's not the perfect plan or, with hindsight, the best tactic to have taken, but by doing something you change your circumstances and start to gain momentum. The key is starting from where you stand right now, not from where you have come from in the past.

All too often people never get started because they have sold themselves on their own story. It usually starts with *because*, which is normally about what has happened to them in the past. The past is the past, and you can learn from it or be tied to it. Using it as the reason why you are where you are in your life is not an option. All the way through this book I have asked you to make decisions; the decision around activity is about starting.

Ritual

Creating a ritual that supports the person you want to become edges you closer to your goals and, even more importantly, assists you every day in feeling how you want to feel. Rituals can build you up and they can tear you down; they can be positive and also negative. Every successful person has a positive ritual that has helped shape their character, qualities and attitudes — almost their personal DNA.

What rituals do you have that generate success and what rituals prevent you from you achieving the very best you? It is your rituals that determine what strength of character you bring to challenges and testing circumstances and how fast you bounce back.

The answer is in this great quote, again from Malcolm McLeod...

'Resilience is born out of consistent rituals!'

What are the rituals that make you stronger — mentally, spiritually and physically?

CHAPTER 32
Defeating the greatest robber of self-esteem

Procrastination, when you know you should do something but you don't do it, is the greatest robber of self-confidence. It eats away at you. You feel bad about *you*. One important enhancer of self-confidence is self-discipline.

I am not talking about running a marathon. It is knowing what needs to be done and doing it. There is no guilt, just the pleasure that comes from making progress, implementing an idea or taking action on something that matters to you. It is the real and pure source of achievement.

Self-discipline sounds like such a tough, no-fun type of word, but it is really about making one decision — do I do it, or do I not do it? If you decide not to do it, then wear the consequences. If it is no big deal, then stop beating yourself up about it and move on!

If you decide to do it, then first of all take the smallest and easiest step possible. It's not about completing it; it's about starting, about gaining some momentum.

Too often we become too focused on completing the task. If you want to beat procrastination forever, then stop thinking about finishing the task and just focus on starting it. The challenge most people have with thinking about finishing the task or project at hand is that there is so much to do, so many steps, so much time needed to make it all come true. Turning it around and just focusing on starting takes all of this thinking out of the picture.

**THE GREATEST ROBBER OF
SELF-CONFIDENCE IS PROCRASTINATION
THE GREATEST ENHANCER OF SELF-CONFIDENCE
IS ACHIEVEMENT.**

A recent participant in one of my Passionate People Programs shared that she had been procrastinating about finishing her master's degree. She had one assignment to complete and the degree was hers. I asked the question: 'What is the first step you need to take?' Her reply was simple: 'Complete the research.' But I disagreed.

Now I have never completed a master's degree, so I could not offer her authoritative advice, but it seemed to me that was too big a task or chunk to start off with. The key is picking something you can do in just five minutes. So my suggestion was first to create a list of the items she needed to research, not to actually do the research.

For her, getting started meant compiling a list of the topics she needed to research, setting herself a deadline for writing the outline of the assignment and booking library time.

When it comes to beating procrastination it is never about finishing; it is only about starting! Don't wait until everything is perfect, START NOW!

Think about it like this...

'A good plan started today is better than a perfect plan started tomorrow. your goal is to get it going, then you can get it right!'

I was giving a presentation in Far North Queensland in a tiered auditorium with over 150 people attending. I did an activity with the group in which they wrote down one task they had been procrastinating over and then noted how long they had been doing so.

I then asked them to put up their hand if they had been procrastinating over that task for more than a week, a month, a year or two years. The longer the time period the fewer hands remained raised, until just one person still had his hand up. So I asked him how long he had been procrastinating over this one task. His answer: 27 years!

I had to ask him if he would mind sharing the task with the group. Sure! Building a barbecue in his backyard, which by the way he had half built already!

People procrastinate over tasks for far longer than it would have taken them to complete the task in the first place. He walked past that half-finished barbecue all those years, constantly reminded of his failure to finish the job.

Maybe you suffer from a similar tendency to defer decisions or actions. This is called *perendinating*. If procrastination is putting off the task until tomorrow, perendinating is putting it off until the day after tomorrow. If procrastination steals self-confidence, then perendinating steals hope. Ultimately it could be an accurate definition for giving up.

When you have no hope, your capacity to dream of what is possible is destroyed. So replace procrastinating and perendinating with being proactive.

Write down one task you are procrastinating over and then write down the smallest step you can take in the next five minutes. Just pick any one action you can do in five minutes to start, whether it's making a call, confirming an appointment, scheduling some planning time or sending an email to reconnect with someone.

By removing items you are procrastinating over you start to remove the crap, clutter and confusion from your life. These three things make us busy rather than productive, producing movement rather than momentum. Procrastination is also the enemy of focus. It's hard to focus on what's important when you are bogged down in the trivial. Sometimes we need to get our base camp in order before we can climb to the summit.

What crap do you need to remove from your life?

What clutter do you need to clean up?

What confusion do you need to gain clarity about?

THE ONLY THING HOLDING YOU BACK FROM FINDING GREATNESS IN YOUR LIFE IS YOU!

CHAPTER 33

Understanding how you like to focus

There are four different ways you receive and recall information:

» visual — through pictures

» auditory — through sounds

» kinaesthetic — through touching and doing

» olfactory — through smell.

For example, certain memories are triggered by smells, such as Grandma's perfume or smells you associate with the home where you grew up.

Here we will focus on the first three areas, as these are the senses you use most when focusing on your goals. Each of us is more dominant in one particular area: this is how we most like to learn and recall. Here is a brief overview, before you complete a quick self-assessment.

Someone with a *visual learning style* has a preference for seen or observed things, including pictures, diagrams, demonstrations, displays, films, flip-charts or handouts. These people will use phrases such as 'show me' and 'let's have a look at that' and will be best able to perform a new task after reading the instructions or watching someone else do it first. They will work from lists and written directions and illustrations.

Have you ever thought about buying a car and the more you think about it, the more examples of this type of car you spot as you drive around? Your reticular activating system has visually tuned in to car images for you.

Someone with an *auditory learning style* absorbs information mainly through listening. These people will use phrases such as 'tell me' and 'let's talk it over' and will be best able to perform a new task after listening to instructions from an expert. They are happy being given spoken instructions over the telephone, and can remember all the words to songs they hear!

Often hearing an old song will immediately take you back to a time in your life when that song meant something to you.

Someone with a *kinaesthetic learning style* has a preference for physical experience — touching, holding, doing, activity, physical movement, hands-on experiences. These people will use phrases such as 'let me try', 'what does it feel like?' and will be best able to perform a new task by going ahead and trying it out, learning as they go. They like to experiment and never look at the instructions first!

You will have memories of learning a skill through movement and physical activity — that is using your senses kinaesthetically.

Of course we all use all of these areas, but each of us tends to have a preferred style. The easiest way to determine your learning style is to complete the VAK Learning Styles Self-Assessment Questionnaire, which can be accessed online (just Google 'VAK Survey' or 'VAK Assessment'); you will be able to complete it online or download a PDF document. It takes you through a bank of a, b and c questions, such as how you might personally ask for directions (by reading a map, asking someone or following your instincts), or how you handle the operation of new equipment, cook new meals or teach someone a new skill. When choosing your answers, go with your first instinct, and remember that no one answer is 'better' than any other. From your results can you determine whether you have a mainly visual, auditory or kinaesthetic learning style?

What has all this got to do with doing what is meaningful in your life? Well, it's simple. When you create a better connection between you and your goal that resonates with your personal makeup, you are likely to have a far greater commitment to that goal. Knowing how you are best able to receive and recall information, and therefore to learn, helps you to focus on what counts in your life, right now.

CHAPTER 34
Focusing on what counts

Whenever you set a goal you will be challenged by distractions, the 'noise' of things that just don't count in the big picture of what you are endeavouring to achieve. If you want to achieve all that you are capable of, *focus* is the core skill you need as part of your DNA.

There are many ways to remain focused on the things that count in your life. Here I'll propose 12 different ideas, which can be classified into three key areas — visual, auditory and kinaesthetic (or V.A.K.). I will share with you some time-proven strategies on how you can remain focused on your key goals using V.A.K. as the formula for focus. That way you can align the focusing techniques with your preferred style of recalling and remembering what is important to you.

Goal focusing techniques

If your preferred learning and recall style is visual, then these visual goal ideas would best suit you:

» **Create a goal board.** Pin pictures of the goals you want to achieve onto a corkboard or whiteboard, and place it somewhere you can see it, review it and focus on it often.

» **Visualise yourself achieving.** Take time out on a regular basis to visualise yourself achieving your goals. It only takes a couple of minutes each day. Picture yourself achieving the successful outcome.

» **Create a visual presentation.** Use your smartphone, tablet or computer to create a presentation of the goals you want to achieve in the year ahead or in your lifetime. Think of it as an electronic goal board. Let's face it, these devices are often your closest companion.

» **Create and publish a photo book.** Many people who have attended our Passionate People workshops use this technique. There are any number of software programs online to help you upload photos, add captions and even print off a hardcopy goal book.

If your preferred learning and recall style is auditory, then you will probably relate better to these ideas:

» **Use a goal card.** Write your goals on a card and read your goal card every day. Put it in your wallet or beside the bed, stick it on the bathroom mirror or on the dashboard of your car. The key is to read it regularly. You can download a goal card from my website www. passionatepeople.com.

» **Discuss your goals with a mentor.** Verbally sharing your goals with a mentor or someone you trust is a great way to gain clarity and focus. Share with them your goal, your thoughts about how you are going to achieve that goal and any challenges you think you may have in the pursuit of that goal.

» **Be still and listen to your intuition.** Spend a few minutes' quiet time each day, closing your eyes and just focusing on one goal. This will bring up thoughts, ideas, strategies. It is an opportunity for you to listen to your inner voice. Note down your ideas and act on them; these are often the ones that will give you the most traction.

» **Listen to interviews.** Research online others who have reached similar goals to those you want to achieve. Most likely there will be podcasts available that describe these people's experiences — how they did it, what they would do differently next time and handy tips that you can learn from in your journey.

If, however, your preferred learning style is kinaesthetic, then you may find these ideas most effective in connecting you with your goals:

» **Meet with inspiring people.** Take the time to meet with people who have achieved similar goals. Their story will inspire and encourage you to keep on working towards the goals you have set for yourself.

» **Experience goal activities.** Testing out or gaining some experience of your goals is a wonderful way to connect with them. For example, if you decide to live in a certain area, drive around that area and visit some house auctions. If you want to study at a certain university, go and do a short course there first.

» **Read inspirational stories.** Be inspired by putting yourself in inspiring environments and submerging yourself in the inspirational stories of people who have already cut a path to the types of goals you want to achieve.

» **Take action.** There is no better feeling than that of making progress. Do something practical each day that brings you closer to your goals.

CHAPTER 35

Stop trying to manage time

I often ask groups of leaders to specify one aspect of their role they need to improve, and someone will always say time management. I normally reply that you can't manage time — that it is impossible to manage something you cannot totally control.

Rather than trying to manage time, manage the priorities that consume your time — those you do have control over. You can choose what to do when and how much time you are going to allocate to completing that priority. So it's not about managing your time, it's about managing your priorities.

The greatest skill you can apply in your life, your career and your business is to determine what is important, what is vital and what gives you the highest payoff for the effort expended. Every day you face different priorities. How you manage them determines your progress each day.

You see, if you don't have any priorities, you will never feel in control, and progress towards your goals will elude you. If you don't set your own priorities, someone else will set them for you and you will be part of their plan, not yours.

In managing priorities you can be reactive, adaptive or proactive.

When you are *reactive* you feel like you have little control or even are out of control. You are always responding to a situation or set of circumstances of someone else's making, which gives you that feeling of always striving but never arriving. If this happens for too long, not only will you feel frustrated, but a sense of hopelessness may also start to creep into your life.

When you are *adaptive* you feel like you have some control and some flexibility in your life to pursue your own goals and interests. Sometimes you have a plan and sometimes you don't. Sometimes things go according to plan and sometimes you must adapt to the circumstances thrown at you. You may feel more puzzled than helpless, wondering why you don't feel in control more often.

When you are *proactive* you feel like you are ahead of the curve. You are doing tasks and activities today for tomorrow. You confidently make your own decisions. Realistically you know not everything will go according to plan, but generally you feel in control of your life, with the ability to stop, regroup, refocus and re-plan as needed.

So how do you become more proactive in your life? Here are eight ideas for bringing out the best in you.

1 Use the right tools

There are so many great online tools and apps available to help you prioritise your day, tasks and projects. You can use a diary or day planner. A tool I created some time ago is simply an A4 page that is divided into four areas ...

» **Projects.** This area is dedicated to helping you to complete the projects you are working on at home or at work that create real momentum in your life. Note down the tasks relating to these projects, including ideas, strategies or specific goals that you need to focus on either personally or professionally.

» **Priorities.** These are the tasks that need to be completed first in the roles you play at work or at home. I work on lots of projects for clients and for my business, so this area makes sense for me. You will have a number of priorities for the week ahead. These will often take the form of promises and commitments you have made to colleagues or customers.

» **Personal.** These tasks relate to your personal goals. If you try to fit them around your busy work schedule, you will always struggle to find time for what is meaningful for your personal life and wellbeing. When planning your week it is important that you allocate time to tasks that move you closer to your personal goals.

» **Pipeline/People/Processes/Proactive.** The fourth area I rename from time to time. One week it could be 'Pipeline', which is about completing sales activities and generating more business for my sales pipeline. One week it could be 'People', which is about managing and working with my team, coaching and mentoring my people better as a leader.

Then it could be 'Processes', which is about how I can streamline my work or business processes to become more effective and efficient. It could also be 'Proactive', which is about working on those long-term tasks that may not show a result in the short term but are vital for the big picture. It's about allocating time to the proactive work required in your specific role or business. An example of this sheet is below, and you can download a PDF version from www.passionatepeople.com.

Weekly plan of action

Week: Month: Year:

Project tasks
Done Day

Priority tasks
Done Day

Pipeline tasks
Done Day

People tasks
Done Day

keithabraham.com

"Plan the plan ... implement the plan ... assess the success ... plan the plan ..." — Keith Abraham CSP

2 Set a time limit

A universal rule is that the task will always expand to fit the time. If you have all day to do something, it will take you all day to complete the task. One of your most productive days may well be the last day before you go on holiday. Most likely you come to work with a plan, a focus, and know exactly what needs to be done to ensure you can go on holiday without having to put out fires while you are away. Why? Because you have a deadline! Be specific: 'I am going to have this part of the project completed by 2 pm today.'

3 Twenty-minute chunks

Twenty minutes of focused attention is better than two hours of distracted attention scattered between a vast number of tasks. Buy yourself an egg timer or use an app on your smartphone and give yourself 20 minutes of uninterrupted time. That means no phone calls, emails or texting, just 100 per cent focus on a single activity or task. Set yourself a goal for the 20 minutes, and then give yourself a reward — five minutes for a coffee or to check those emails or return any calls you have missed. For some people this will be a challenge, as everyone now believes we need to be digitally connected 24/7.

Every goal or project is made up of a series of small steps. Focus on your goal but be clear about your next step. The ancient Chinese philosopher Lao Tzu said ...

'Great acts are made up of small deeds.'

We all marvel at the achievements of some people, yet the greatest achievements can be broken down into a series of little steps applied with tenacity over time. Think of a goal you want to achieve and now think of three small action steps you need to take this month, and one action step you could take in the next three hours, to bring the goal closer.

4 Give yourself time

You need to give yourself time to recharge. One per cent of 24 hours is roughly 15 minutes. You give time to your work, customers, family, friends and community groups — when is there time for you? At the end of the day, when you have nothing left to give? To do everything you want to do, you need time and space for mental maintenance. This is a great time to refocus yourself or just to be still and take some quiet time to meditate. If you are always running on an adrenaline-fuelled high, then when do you give yourself time to stop and recalibrate?

5 Clean out the clutter

Clutter can be one of the core sources of stress and confusion in your life. Have a big cleanout of your desk, office, cupboards, garage and even your wardrobe. Release yourself from the accumulation of *stuff*. Streamline your life by looking at what you can do to set yourself free from the clutter. Pick a day in the next seven to ten days and pick one area of your life to de-clutter.

6 Save minutes

All too often people are looking to save hours and it is the wrong focus. Look at activities and actions you can take to save minutes. To put this into perspective, saving 10 minutes each day means recovering 60 hours in a year — a full working week to devote to a project, person or program, or to *you*. Review where you consume time in your life and work. It could be email, paperwork, travelling time or meetings you attend or run. Then decide how to save minutes. Look at what efficiency processes you could create and find out from others what they do to save time in these areas.

7 Tackle the tough task first

Complete the toughest task first and everything else becomes easier. There are always going to be necessary actions and tasks you won't want to do — tasks that seem especially big and challenging. My suggestion is do them first. If you don't, over time they seem to become bigger in your mind. Most likely you are thinking about it all day as you work on other tasks, rather than actually doing something about it. In other words, you have given it all of your mental attention but not your physical attention. A funny thing about tackling the toughest task first is it's never as big as you thought it was!

8 Prioritise

Not all priorities are equal. Generally your priorities will fall into one of three categories: *must do, should do* and *could do,* or A, B and C priorities. An A priority must be done today. It is vital, mission critical. Ignore it and you could lose a customer, let down a friend or cost yourself money. It will also reflect poorly on you in your role.

A B priority is important. If you got it done today, you are being proactive. It is not required today, but if you do complete it, you are forward planning and preparing — getting ahead of the curve, so to speak.

A C priority tends to be nice to do, but it's not a big deal if you don't get it done today. No-one is relying on it being completed immediately, but a C priority today could become an A priority in three or four days' time.

It is never about time. It's about what you do with the time you have. All of us have the same 24-hour daily allocation, so how do some people achieve so much and others so little? The answer lies in how they manage their priorities.

CHAPTER 36
Recharging your batteries

It is hard to achieve what you want to if you don't have sufficient reserves of energy. You can always do more in the time you have if you have great energy. Energy gives us the ability to do more with what we have. When you devote energy in the areas that are important to you, you create energy to spend elsewhere in your life.

I believe we all have an internal battery that needs to be regularly recharged to replenish and re-energise us. This recharging is not something you do only if it fits into your busy schedule. It is something you need to do regularly and deliberately.

The activities we engage in have the capacity to recharge our mind, re-energise our body and replenish our spirit. It is also true that there are certain activities we engage in that create chaos in our life and detract from all we are trying to achieve.

There are four core ways in which we can build our energy levels to help us achieve our goals.

Do what you love to do

The first can be summed up in the message returned to again and again throughout this book — *pursue your passion!* When you are doing what you love to do you gain more energy. I will take energy over time any day, because I can do more with the time I have if I have greater levels of energy.

In your life there will be things you like to do, things you have to do and from time to time even things you hate to do that may nonetheless be unavoidable. However, you owe it to yourself and to the people who mean the world to you that you also do the things that give you joy and purpose.

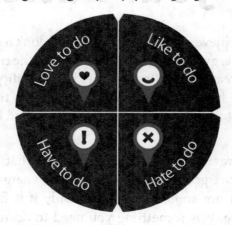

It is this act of giving back to yourself that provides you with the energy to tackle the tasks you find uncomfortable or inconvenient. People who are most unhappy are not following their heart, pursuing their passion by doing the activities that give them joy.

Eat wisely

Some ways to generate energy are obvious to most people. What you eat and drink affects your energy levels. Eating foods that are right for my body, taking a little extra care to select the healthiest options, contributes to my high energy levels. Now I am not a health food junkie, but I do know what works for me. Does that mean I am a perfect eater? No. I still treat myself to my favourite types of food once a week.

Drink what you need to

Often when we think we are hungry we may actually be thirsty. Do you measure how much water you drink each day? Find out what the right amount is for you. Book an appointment with a nutritionist to find out what foods are right for you and how much water you should be drinking. Not what the average person should be drinking — you are definitely not average! Each of us has one body to carry us through life. Why not learn how to get the best results from it?

Exercise your body

The physical exercise you do on a regular basis will also have a big impact on your energy levels. This is not about running a marathon each day but about moving and improving your body. Exercise generates energy and with energy you can do so much more. Talk to a personal trainer or your local gym and have them design a program that is right for your age, weight and current level of fitness. It is marvellous what happens when you lose a couple of surplus kilos you have been carrying around — you have energy to burn for the things that count for you.

Work out what is right for you and decide what you need to do to gain the energy to achieve all that you are capable of in your lifetime.

CHAPTER 37

Rituals create your future

As discussed in chapter 31, people create rituals and rituals form futures. It is so simple and true. If you don't have the future you have dreamt about, it is most likely because you have not had in place the habits or rituals you need to create the future you desire. Everything we have achieved or not achieved is a result of the rituals we have that either propel us forward or hold us back.

A ritual is an activity you engage in on a regular and consistent basis. The difference between the successes of individuals rests on the combination of successful rituals they apply. When I have interviewed successful leaders a common comment comes up: 'I have always done this ...'

The challenge for each of us is to define the rituals that best support us in our pursuit of our dreams, desires, goals and passion, while also identifying the rituals that act as roadblocks. In identifying the roadblock rituals, we need to shift our thinking from *unconsciously incompetent* (not knowing what rituals are not supporting you) to *consciously incompetent* (actually knowing what you need to improve and creating the right ritual for you).

'YOUR RITUALS CAN BE
ROADBLOCKS OR RAMPS.'

To identify the non-supportive rituals, you need to sit down and focus on what does not assist you in becoming the best you that you can be. Once identified, determine what the opposite to that ritual is for you.

It could be that not exercising is a ritual that does not support your feeling fit and energised, so the ritual you need to adopt is to move your body daily through some type of exercise. The key is to create rituals that lift your spirit, making you feel the best you that you can be, and that generate positive proactive results. If you struggle to identify what you need to improve, you may need to work with a coach and a mentor as you journey towards your goals.

The second strategy is to identify how you want to feel. Review your driving emotions, the top three feelings you want to achieve. Then build a set of rituals around them.

For example, your three driving emotions could be *energised*, *successful* and *impactful*. The table below could include some of the rituals you would need to engage in each day to generate how you want to feel. The amount of water you drink, the types of foods you eat and the exercise you complete would all contribute to your levels of energy. By completing three key objectives and connecting with seven clients each day you would generate the feeling of success. Being still and reflecting on what you are grateful for or a lesson you have learned would also have an impact on your positive attitude.

MY DAILY RITUALS

HOW I WANT TO FEEL: Energised	Successful			Impactful			
	MON	TUE	WED	THU	FRI	SAT	SUN
2–3 Litres of Water	✓	✓	✓	✓	✓	✓	✓
60 Minutes of Exercise	✓	✓		✓	✓		✓
Complete 3 Objectives	✓	✓	✓	✓			
Eat Clean Food & Vitamins	✓	✓	✓	✓	✓	✓	✓
Connect with 7 Clients	✓	✓		✓	✓		
Create Something New	✓	✓		✓		✓	
Be Still for 15–30 Minutes		✓	✓	✓	✓		✓

I recommend that you develop at least two rituals for each emotion you want to experience each day. That way if you do not complete one ritual you may be able to complete the other and still experience the emotion.

You can use this as a checklist to measure your progress while working towards creating that perfect day of rituals. I am a realist and know it won't always go to plan, but if you have no plan then you leave it to chance. I would rather be deliberate, choose the plan and action that plan until the rituals I require become the habits I desire.

I know I am mentally tougher and more resilient when I exercise, eat well, meditate and connect with people. It is this conscious progress that sends a message to your resistance that you will not be held captive by your past.

Start off small. What is one habit that you need to implement in your daily life, that you know is in line with your goals and how you want to feel? To begin with it is not about being disciplined in multiple areas, but about making a start and taking small steps.

Sample rituals

Here are 15 examples of rituals that can help you connect emotionally, mentally and physically.

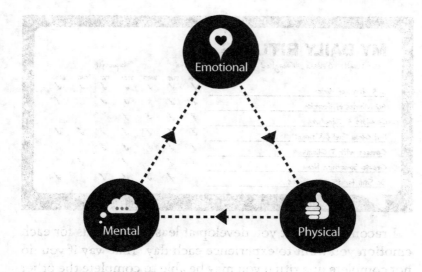

EMOTIONAL RITUALS

1. Visualise yourself achieving your goals.
2. Review your goal journal.
3. Look at the goal board of your key goals.
4. Listen to your intuition.
5. Really connect with people you love.

MENTAL RITUALS

1. Meditate for 15 to 30 minutes daily.
2. Read books that inspire and inform you, giving you greater insights.
3. Listen to positive audio recordings.
4. Start the day with a goal and a plan.
5. Reflect on what worked, what didn't and what you are going to do differently.

PHYSICAL RITUALS

1. Exercise on a regular basis.

2. Eat the right foods for you and your body.

3. Network with positive people.

4. Drink two litres of water a day.

5. Complete one key goal a day.

My belief is that rather than waiting until the goal is achieved, why not experience that feeling today? You want to feel and then do what makes you feel great. Habits and rituals are vital if you want to create what is most important to you and to be consistent in your life.

CHAPTER 38
1% improvements

The fact is that to achieve all you are capable of achieving you are going to need to change. You have to become the living example of the person you need to be to achieve the goals and create the life you desire. Change is not always easy; in fact, it is often uncomfortable and inconvenient. However, what sets people who become truly significant in their lives apart from people who merely survive is that they change before they need to, before they have to or are made to change.

When it comes to change you have two choices. You can be the ...

"Victim of change or the catalyst for change"

When you are the victim, change happens to you and around you, it challenges you and you react to it. If you avoid it, change *will* bite you.

As a catalyst you are also challenged by change, but to become the person you need to be to achieve your goals you have to be proactive. You have to tackle change head on, accepting that you well be uncomfortable and inconvenienced along the way. To obtain control over change you first need to be a catalyst for change.

Victims spend their energy complaining about change, wishing it never happened, thinking of ways to hide from it. They remember 'the good old days'. Catalysts, on the other hand, spend their energy looking for the opportunities and possibilities, and thinking about what they need to do to be better equipped in handling the change.

You can think of change as revolution or as evolution. If you don't change you could face a revolution that turns your whole world upside down. However, an evolution is made up of small, deliberate, incremental changes created over time. In other words, you just need to make small 1 per cent changes. I call them 1 per cent ideas.

One global company that does this exceptionally well is Toyota. Over the past 10 years that I have been fortunate enough to work with Toyota, one of my main insights about the organisation is that they have a wonderful culture of change. Part of the Toyota Way is the principle of *kaizen* or continuous improvement.

As part of my education on how Toyota operate I read their bible, called *The Toyota Way*, which explains their philosophy and DNA. But it was not until I visited their factory in Nagoya, Japan, that I fully understood the process of kaizen. I was watching the car manufacturing process from above the production line. Each car started out as a metal shell and progressed along the production line, stopping at each work station where a team of people attached a series of parts and installed components until it was eventually transformed into a complete car and driven off the production line, bound for one of Toyota's global markets.

As interesting as this process was, it was something else I noticed happening on the production line that really caught my eye. Every now and then one of the workers would write something on the whiteboard located in their work area. During the course of my visit I noticed this happen five or six times. Intrigued, I asked our guide what was going on. He explained they were encouraged to write down any ideas for possible improvement that occurred to them.

'How many ideas do the workers generate each year?' I asked. Each year Toyota's 60 000 employees worldwide propose more than 900 000 ideas to improve their business — that's just over one idea a month, or 15 ideas per person per year, and about 97 per cent of them are implemented within 12 months.

How can you implement so many ideas in a year? Their secret is simple: they are 1 per cent ideas. The implementation of small steps, ideas, solutions and strategies, when joined together, can make a huge difference in your life, family, career and business.

Identify what you need to improve and then ask yourself, 'What step do I need to take to improve that area by 1 per cent?'

To achieve all that you are capable of achieving, you are going to have to do some things differently. You will need to make small, incremental changes over time that will carry you closer to your *why*. The smaller the change and the faster you implement it, the less pain you will experience.

One of my clients Tony Wood, offered this thought to me...

'Pace over perfection.'

It is a great message for each of us. So often we wait until everything is perfect before we even attempt to get started on achieving our goals. Let's face facts, the circumstances will rarely be perfect, but start anyway. When you start to change you don't need perfection, you need to create momentum.

Many people talk about change being difficult when in fact it is just different. Here's what I mean: Right now cross your arms. Which arm is on top — right or left? Now fold your arms again, but this time put the opposite arm on top. How did it feel? It wasn't difficult, just different. It's the same when you want to become better in your life: you will need to change some things. Those changes will seem difficult but in reality they are just different.

The more things you do differently, the quicker you will get to your goals. Whenever you challenge your status quo you will be uncomfortable.

LIMIT YOURSELF TO WHAT IS COMFORTABLE & YOU LIMIT YOURSELF TO WHAT IS POSSIBLE.

What a great quote!

Where are you playing it safe?

Where are you limiting yourself?

What is possible for you to change — today, this week or this month?

Life is meant to be enjoyable and uncomfortable as we each pursue our passion, goals and dreams. So think of it like this: if you are uncomfortable, you are most likely exploring your possibilities!

The one thing you need to be aware of is that as you change you will be tested. Life has a funny way of checking to see if you are serious about changing. Sometimes there is no pathway or even a signpost to give you direction.

Sometimes you have to blaze a new path. I don't mean that it has never been done before. I just mean it is new to you, a journey you have not taken before or perhaps it has been a long time since you have attempted it.

I heard this recently and thought it was a great way to describe the journey we have to take as we pursue our passions and achieve our goals ...

'YOU MAY HAVE TO PAVE THE ROAD BEHIND YOU.'

You may have to be the living example, the explorer, to start without a map, not knowing what will happen next, to figure it out as you go along.

Just start!

CHAPTER 39
Bringing it all together

Bringing together all the ideas we have covered in this book means reviewing eight key elements that will help you to summarise what you can do and how you can start to create momentum.

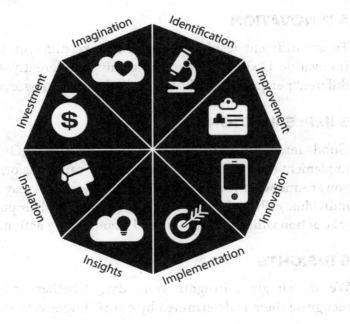

1 IMAGINATION

Throughout this book I have urged you to use your imagination to create a vision, a reason, your *why*. This is the catalyst for a new beginning. If you aren't already, become clear of your vision.

2 IDENTIFICATION

Once you know where you want to be, you can determine your direction and path. Start from where you are now. Don't wait for everything to be perfect in your mind or life, just start.

3 IMPROVEMENT

As we spoke about in the last chapter, it is about making small, incremental improvements over time. What may seem like an insignificant action, when combined with other small acts applied with a tenacious spirit, can generate great change.

4 INNOVATION

To get different results you need to take different actions. Innovation is simply about doing things differently. Gain a different perspective to shift your thinking to a new level.

5 IMPLEMENTION

Good intentions will never change anything. Only the implementation of ideas through action can transform who you are and what you achieve. As simplistic as this may sound, individuals who achieve greatness and tap into their potential take action while others only think about taking action.

6 INSIGHTS

We are all given insights every day. Whether or not we recognise them is determined by our willingness to stop and reflect, to take time out of our busy, crazy and demanding schedules to be still, listen and see. Insights have an impact on our foresight; they shape how we think today about what we want to achieve tomorrow.

7 INSULATION

Not everything will go your way. There will be negative results and negative people who may not have the same amount of optimism as you have for your future. They could be friends, family members or colleagues. If you are not sure how to recognise the negative people, the answer is simple: when they leave you, do you feel better? Insulate yourself from negative people who don't support your vision, goals and passion. It's not about abandoning them, but about not being influenced by them.

8 INVESTMENT

To achieve all you are capable of, you need to invest time, energy, effort, heart and money. Everyone wants to be successful, to achieve the best results for themselves and their family. Everyone wants the best. The real test, however, is whether you are prepared to invest in your future success. That is when you communicate to the world that you are serious. You are worth it!

When you combine all eight of these elements, a certain type of magic comes to you. It is hard to explain, almost surreal, but it does work.

CHAPTER 40
The first domino

You may have seen a domino show on TV, where a vast and complex arrangement of dominoes has been laboriously set up, normally in a shopping centre, in anticipation of the great moment when someone pushes the first domino, setting off a massive chain reaction of falling dominos.

This chapter is devoted to determining your first domino — that first action that will create momentum in your life. I really appreciate your reading this book, but the real value of the ideas, concepts and philosophies it contains can only be truly realised if you do something with these insights.

It can be so easy to believe our own story — I am too busy now; I'll just wait until things settle down before I start; I need more information; I need to gain the support of a few friends before I launch; I need to get a nest egg together before I can really get into it.

Everything we do or don't do has a cost. I like Seth Godin's take on this, though...

'The cost of being wrong is less than the cost of doing nothing.'

How often do we not do something because of the fear of being wrong? At what stage in our life did we come to accept the idea that we need to be perfect at everything we do? That we need to achieve our goals without failure, without facing challenges and with everything going to plan?

In the real world, sometimes we need to be wrong — not deterred, just wrong. We need to take risks, put ourselves out there, live on the edge and try things that we will not master at our first attempt. We need to push our comfort zone to get ahead. You will be amazed at what you are capable of if you take a few chances!

Look at it this way, what if everything that has challenged you, all the problems you have faced, the disappointments you have experienced and the setbacks you have endured, what if they were supposed to happen to you? What if these challenges were just tests, a way of preparing you for something greater, a quest that you are not yet even aware of?

This is my way of putting things into real perspective when things in my life are not going the way I planned. I just say to myself...

'Everything is perfect!'

It is my way of shifting my mindset and emotional state from victim (Why is this happening to me?) to catalyst (What new opportunities and possibilities does this situation offer?).

If everything is perfect in your life right now, then what are you going to do next?

The Japanese have an expression, *Wabi-sabi*, which refers to the acceptance of imperfection and the idea of beauty as imperfect, impermanent and incomplete. As much as we might try, you and I are not and can never be perfect.

However, that is just perfect. Once we accept that things, circumstances and situations may not turn out as we planned or expected, we can turn our attention to our intention rather than burning up useless energy on trying to be right, perfect and complete.

Trying to work out why it did not work or why 'it always happens to me' is a waste of energy and effort. You need to look for what you can learn from these circumstances. That process becomes the catalyst for each of us to change.

Ask yourself these three questions:

» What is not perfect in my life?

» What is the message for me?

» What am I going to do about it?

In answering these questions, you acquire a unique mindset, which will enable you to create momentum in your life.

I read a great quote recently ...

'The sign of your real character is who turns up when the sun is not shining.'

We can all be great, positive and upbeat when things are perfect, but the best predictor of success is turning up, fronting up and being upbeat when times are tough. That's the test of true character. Who do you want to turn up and represent you when the going gets tough?

Without action, nothing changes, nothing is achieved. What is the first domino for you?

What is one action you are going to take in the next 24 hours?

What is one goal you are going to achieve in the next seven days?

What are you going to achieve in the next 14 days?

What are you going to have achieved within the next 30 days?

CONCLUSION
Become the living example

There was a mother in India who had tried everything to stop her child from eating chocolate all of the time. With every option exhausted she finally took her little boy to see Mahatma Gandhi. After standing in line for hours she was at last able to speak to him. She explained her challenge and Gandhi listened intently.

The great man pondered for a moment then asked the woman to take the boy away and come back in 30 days' time. The woman did not expect that advice and didn't understand his rationale, but she followed his instructions. Thirty days later she returned with her son. Gandhi looked the boy in the eye with a piercing stare and after a few moments of silence he said:

'Give up chocolate and don't eat it anymore unless your mother says so!'

After the boy had walked away, never to eat chocolate again, his mother asked Gandhi why he had waited a month to give that advice. Gandhi's reply was simple: 'I had to give up eating chocolate first.'

You can talk about your goals, plan out your goals and dream big dreams, but once you have done this you need to become the living example of a person worthy, capable and deserving of achieving your goals by applying the right mindset, creating a plan and knowing why you want that goal in the first place.

All the way through this book I have spoken about the emotional, mental and physical aspects of goal alignment. Only by combining all three can you gain true alignment and an unbreakable connection with your goals. So I can think of no better way to conclude this book than using these three components to share with you three ways to become the living example in your life.

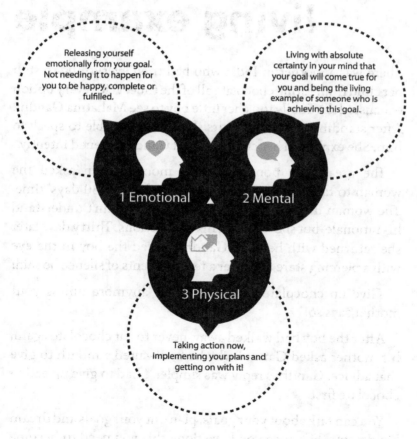

Releasing yourself emotionally from your goal. Not needing it to happen for you to be happy, complete or fulfilled.

Living with absolute certainty in your mind that your goal will come true for you and being the living example of someone who is achieving this goal.

1 Emotional   2 Mental

3 Physical

Taking action now, implementing your plans and getting on with it!

Emotional connection

We are emotional creatures; our ability to express our emotions verbally is one thing that separates human beings from all other creatures. The emotional connection is the foundation of our reasoning for why we want to achieve a certain goal. Here are three key strategies to keep close to your heart as you become the living example ...

DETERMINE HOW YOU WANT TO FEEL

Before you set your goal, work out how you want to feel and then ask yourself, 'Will that goal and action generate this feeling?' If it won't, then the goal is not right for you. This one connection can manifest many goals for you in your life. It is the missing link, the element that can have the greatest impact. Just imagine experiencing your driving emotions every day. What influence would that have on your mindset? What impact would it have on the amount of momentum you are able to create? Your emotion is the fuel that propels you more quickly to your goals.

LET GO

There comes a time when you have to let go of the goal, which means you need to release yourself from the goal emotionally. Emotional power is also about having the ability to let things go, to free yourself from worry, doubt and the demanding expectations that consume you. All too often people want to achieve their goal so badly that they become consumed by it. Let go of your goal, confident that it will come true because you have a plan and you are taking action to bring it closer to you.

BE INSPIRING

To be inspiring, you need to be inspired. You need to be deliberate about putting yourself in inspiring environments and determined to find ways to recharge your energy, your passion and your spirit. Life, and people for that matter, can sometimes wear you down so it is critical that you do the things you love to do, engage in activities that make a difference and find ways to pursue your passions. If you are inspired, you automatically become a living example for those people who are close to you, and perhaps even for people you have never even met.

Mental connection

Mental power is about having a resilient attitude, an attitude that combats the resistance to change for the better, being able to see through the rationale for maintaining the status quo. Here are three ways to shift your thinking...

CHANGE YOUR LANGUAGE

The words you use make a difference. If you want to change, then change the way you speak to yourself. Move your language patterns from 'I will *try*' to 'I *will* do it', from 'I *think*' to 'I *believe*' ('I believe this is right for me'), from '*Some day*...' to '*When*...' ('When I achieve my goal'), from '*could*' to '*can*' ('I can do that'), from '*how*' to '*why*' ('Why I want to achieve my goal').

STOP WORRYING

In their book *Rework*, Jason Fried and David Heinemeier Hansson write...

> 'When you spend time worrying about someone else, you can't spend that time improving yourself.'

What other people think about you is none of your business. Live up to your own expectations. Life is too short to be always looking over your shoulder. Don't seek approval from others when the only approval you need is your own. Instead, channel your energy into taking action and celebrate the fact that you are moving forward.

BE HAPPY NOW

How often do you play the 'as soon as' game — as soon as this customer makes a decision, as soon as the kids go to school full time, as soon as I get this deal across the line, as soon as I get this promotion or as soon as this person becomes the boss, things will be better? Socrates said it best:

'He who is not content with what he has would not be content with what he would like to have.'

You need to find the gift in your current situation. You need to find the positive outcome and the joy right now! That is not to say that you shouldn't seek to do better, be better and have better results, but I see too many people wish their life away rather than enjoying the moment. Not everything will go to plan, but you will have more positive, memorable moments when you find joy in the moment.

Physical connection

Life is never about what you intend to do but is measured only by what you have done and are doing right now. To create the physical connection to your goal you need to take action and get on with it!

DON'T WAIT FOR THE RIGHT MOMENT

All too often people wait and wait for the right moment to start. My advice is to start from where you stand, start now and take action quickly. Decide that it is not what happens to you or what has happened to you that counts, but how you respond to it. Viktor Frankl, author of *Man's Search for Meaning*, wrote ...

'Between stimulus & response there is a space. In that space is our power to choose our response. In our response lies our growth & our freedom.'

How often do we feel upset, stressed, worried or threatened by a situation that will not matter in the least in a month's time or even tomorrow? When you are controlled by a set of circumstances it is difficult to take the action you need to move forward. Choose your response and you choose your destiny!

PAY THE PRICE

Action is the price you need to pay to achieve your goals. Henry David Thoreau wrote, 'The price of anything is the amount of life you exchange for it.'

What price are you prepared to pay to pursue your passions? I don't mean in dollars and cents, but in time and energy. Maybe a better question is, how much is it costing you to *not* do what you love? What mindset is being created, what messages are you sending to others and what habits are being formed as you engage in activities that don't lead you towards your goals?

You will always pay a price in time, money or energy — just make sure it's a price for which you gain a full return.

ACT FASTER

What is the worst that can happen as you get closer to the right answer, action or goal? In a post-retirement interview, former CEO of General Electric Jack Welsh was asked, if he could have his time over again what would he do differently? His reply:

'Think bigger, act faster!'

I particularly like the part about acting faster. Sometimes I think I take too long to act, waiting for the right moment or better circumstances. Does this apply to you? It costs little or nothing to dream bigger and in the long run it is less costly to act faster.

It's often said that we underestimate how much we can do in a lifetime and overestimate what we can get done in a year. Make a decision, move forward and if it is not the right one, make another one. Make progress as you pursue your passion.

THE 9 NON-NEGOTIABLE STEPS TO A PASSIONATE LIFE

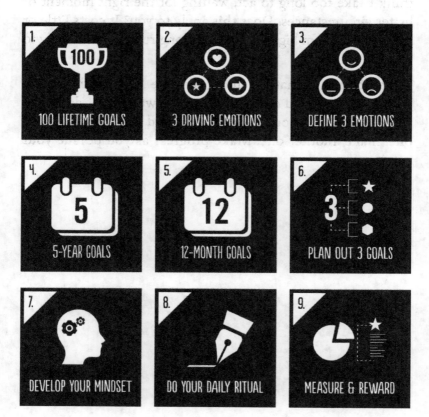

For a quick summary of what to do next to create the life you have dreamed about, to do what matters, what makes a difference, and to become the living example of the person you desire to be, here are the nine non-negotiable steps to a passionate life:

1. Write down your 100 lifetime goals.

2. Identify your three driving emotions.

3. Define what each of these emotions truly means to you.

4. Determine what you want to achieve in the next five years.

5. Decide what you want to achieve in the next 12 months.

6. Select one to three goals and plan them out in detail.

7. Move your mindset by developing your self-esteem, self-confidence and self-belief.

8. Complete a daily ritual in order to generate how you want to feel.

9. Measure and reward your progress and learning experiences.

Thank you for taking the time to read this book. May all your dreams come true while you pursue your passion and live a life that matters.

Ideas–insights–information–inspiration

In these pages Keith has included a range of our Passionate Performance Inc. resources, tools and information that can assist you on your journey towards achieving your goals.

One Goal Global challenge™—Set a goal, share a goal, gift a goal!

The real power of goal setting is not what goal you achieve, but what happens to you on the journey towards the goal. It is just as true for most of us that when a goal is achieved without anyone to celebrate it with, it can be a hollow victory. The real joy comes when we make a difference in the pursuit of that goal — a difference in our own life and a difference to others.

One Goal Global Challenge™ is the catalyst that combines each of these three elements so you can achieve more for yourself, inspire those people who mean the world to you and make a difference to others by leaving a legacy that is worth talking about and being proud of.

What if you set a goal for yourself, be it big or small in your eyes. Then you shared it with someone who matters. Nothing like being accountable to follow through. Then as part of this journey you assist someone in need to achieve one of their goals through a small $1 *Global Goal Gift* to the Passionate Performance Inc. Foundation.

We believe what the world needs now is more passionate people who are prepared to make their world better by being better themselves and sharing their success with others. Like to make a global difference? Head to www. onegoalglobalchallenge.com and click on One Goal Global Challenge.

Passionate People app

Everything outlined in this book is fundamentally about following a process to achieve your goals. To assist in this process Passionate Performance Inc. has created an app for your iPhone, iPad, BlackBerry and android smartphone devices.

iPhone and iPad:

Open up the App Store, and search for 'Passionate People'.

BlackBerry:

https://appworld.blackberry.com

Android:

https://play.google.com/store/apps

Once you have downloaded the app onto your device, you can create a personal profile with a username and password. Use your email address as your username (it is case sensitive). You can now begin to create your list of lifetime dreams, set your key goals, use the *Feel — Think — Do* process, upload a photo of your goal, and share your goals on Facebook or Twitter. If you need assistance, there is also a HELP tab.

Keith Abraham's blog

Three times a week Keith writes blog posts that relate directly to how you can follow your dreams and live with passion, doing what matters, what is meaningful and what makes a difference. It is packed full of insights, inspiration and ideas to support you on your journey.

You can sign up at www.keithabrahamblog.com.

Passionate Performance Inc. community website

On our website, www.passionateperformanceinc.com, you will be able to access a host of videos, podcasts, articles and information to assist you in the pursuit of your dreams, goals and passion. You will find the 100 Goal Challenge details and can choose your favourite way to stay socially connected.

Passionate People Program information

At the core of every achievement is someone with a passion! At Passionate Performance Inc. we believe the Passionate People Program offers real benefits in assisting individuals to tap into that passion by reconnecting to what is important, what matters, what is meaningful and what makes a difference in their lives.

This program can also be the foundation that supports all your organisation's leadership, professional development, sales and service programs. As you can appreciate, it is difficult to create a high-performance culture that leads to significant shifts in mindsets when your people are not transforming themselves in their own lives and careers.

The purpose of this program is to assist your people to:

» create a stronger sense of personal and professional certainty so they find greater meaning when undertaking the work that matters

» gain clarity about the personal and professional milestones they need to achieve to make the most valuable contribution to your business and their own family

» become more confident as a person within their role, your business and their industry

» be consistent in their approach, attitude and actions so they create greater momentum in their personal life and business role

» recognise that the foundation of every achievement is the ability to focus on your key goals.

At the end of this program, your passionate people will:

» inspire the people around them to be better, do better and achieve better results as they become the living example of a passionate, positive and professional team member

» become confident and competent to take initiative in their role, laying the foundation for a culture of innovation, implementation and improvement

» move their mindset so they can be more focused in their approach to solving problems and leading teams of proactive problem solvers

» create the time and space to use their mental muscle to implement ideas, strategies and initiatives in a way that transforms the very nature of their team and your business.

The program model

Meaningful ...

Everyone needs to find meaning in what they do and in the role they play. As team members, we need to understand the connection and alignment of what we do in our day-to-day role, the company's strategic objectives and our personal goals. When people identify their personal and professional reasons for achievement, the by-product is laser-like focus.

Milestones ...

Dreams and desires are the foundation, but it is the clarity that comes from clearly defined milestones that truly transitions intentions into actions. What is measurable becomes maintainable. The clarity of each person's milestones enables them to measure their progress and impact.

Mindset ...

Rarely is it a person's ability or capability that stops them from achieving their goals. Most often it is their lack of confidence and belief in what's possible that creates the roadblock. Your people need to become living examples of people who are certain, have clarity and believe in their ability to achieve the desired results, both personally and professionally.

Momentum ...

Your people don't only need to be motivated, they need to create personal and professional momentum through taking action, focused priorities, managing distractions and working on projects that generate real progress. Team members today need to master what not to do, rather than trying to do everything.

People find it far easier to set business goals than personal goals, yet the personal goals are the real reasons for them to go the extra mile.

The real program benefits

The Passionate People Program offers a number of benefits for both your organisation and your people. The two key areas are greater employee engagement and enhanced individual wellness.

Employee engagement

Recent research found that in most companies only 18 per cent of the workforce were *actively engaged*, 61 per cent were *not engaged* and 21 per cent were *actively disengaged*. Here are some specific company benefits that we have identified from past groups we have worked with on the Passionate People Program:

» Team members increase their discretionary effort.

» Greater retention is a by-product of investing in the individual rather than just the employee.

» When people are happy in life, they are more productive at work.

» Attendance increases as people feel better about themselves, their role and your business.

» Individuals bring more energy and passion to their job.

» Positive people equals a positive employer brand.

Individual wellness

With physical and mental health issues on the rise around the world, the Passionate People Program plays a part in individual overall wellness. People feel different, act better and manifest a more positive outlook when they:

» have a greater sense of personal direction in their life

» can align their personal purpose with the opportunities provided by your organisation

» identify the contribution and difference they are making through their working role

» recognise that their career can be a vehicle to achieving their personal goals

» find greater meaning in what they do personally and professionally

» feel better and look at ways to improve themselves further and achieve better results in all areas of life.

If you would like additional information on how the Passionate People Program can transform your workforce, then please email your request to inquiry@passionateperformanceinc.com.

Conference speaking services

For the past 27 years Keith has researched, designed and developed personal and professional development programs around the globe. He has always been dedicated to delivering substance that relates to the real world in which we live. Increasingly he has been drawn to the cause of showing people how to do what they love and love what they do, assisting them to find, pursue and live their passion. Most importantly, his strategies have produced proven, phenomenal results for companies and individuals right around the world.

The founder of Passionate Performance Inc., Keith believes his purpose is to create an everlasting legacy that will make a profound difference to people's lives. He has also written the best-selling books *Creating Loyal Profitable Customers* and *Living Your Passion*. He is a regular contributor to business magazines and industry journals and is a regular guest on *Grow Your Business* on Fox TV in Australia.

GET SOCIAL!

f facebook.com/KeithAbrahamCSP
g+ plus.google.com *search* Keith Abraham
▶ youtube.com/KeithAbraham1
🐦 twitter.com/keithlabraham

Special thanks

To write a book like the one you have just read, it takes a team of people who believe in what you do, support you and want to see you become successful. I have been very fortunate to have a great team of people around me who helped bring my sketchy ideas into reality.

Dorratt Design

To Brooke and Aimie Dorratt, who are two creative geniuses who take concepts and content and turn them into images and illustrations that have given a totally different dynamic dimension to this book, thank you for being there with me on this journey over the past nine years.

www.dorrattdesign.com.au

Juliette Tobias-Webb

Thanks, Juliette, for all the wonderful research you did during the course of writing this book. I appreciate the way you always looked for a different angle and went beyond the immediate scope of the subject to find material that was insightful and informative.

Melissa Williscroft

Melissa, I greatly appreciate your taking the time to proofread my work before we passed it to my editor. I have always been a great believer in virtual assistants and you truly are one of the best in the game. Thank you for your prompt and efficient service.

www.mjsvirtual.com.au

Malcolm McLeod

Thank you, Mal, for pushing my thinking in the areas of speaking and writing. I am so grateful that you have been in my corner all these years. Everyone needs a buddy like you to share meaningful conversations that challenge the status quo one minute then switch to a totally unrelated topic the next.

You are a great friend and I love you like a brother!

www.handwritingguy.com.au

Wiley

Every great business is made up of great people. This book started in New York with a lunch I had with Matt Holt. Thanks, Matt, for listening to my idea, for your ongoing support and for believing in the work I do. To Kristen Hammond, who I have worked with closely throughout this project, thank you for your encouragement, understanding and the gentle way in which you have brought out the best in me. It was wonderful having you assist me as I navigated my way through the book writing, editing, publishing and marketing process for this special book.

www.wiley.com

Karen Phillips — Karen Phillips Corporate Communications

When I first learnt about goal setting almost 30 years ago, Karen was at that RYLA Program as a participant, like myself. She has been a wonderful friend for all of these years and has been instrumental in assisting me to clarify and build my brand. Karen has played an amazing role in bringing this book to life. I am deeply grateful for having her in my corner not only during this project but for all of my adult life. Her friendship, understanding and expertise has been one of the greatest gifts I have ever been given.

www.karenphillips.com.au

Ian Andrew

I have had the great pleasure to work with some wonderful clients over the past few decades — clients who are always willing to assist me, if I need a helping hand. One person who has always been willing and able is Ian Andrew. He has been willing to give input, thoughts, suggestions and in this case, time to proofread my book. Thanks Ian, I really appreciate your assistance.